Greece & R

NEW SURVEYS IN THE (

RECEPTION STUDIES

BY

LORNA HARDWICK

Published for the Classical Association

OXFORD UNIVERSITY PRESS

2003

OXFORD

UNIVERSITY PRESS

Great Clarendon Street, Oxford OX2 6DP

Oxford University Press is a department of the University of Oxford
and furthers the University's aim of excellence in research, scholarship,
and education by publishing worldwide in

Oxford New York

Athens Auckland Bangkok Bogotá Bombay Buenos Aires Calcutta
Cape Town Chennai Dar es Salaam Delhi Florence Hong Kong Istanbul
Karachi Kuala Lumpur Madrid Melbourne Mexico City Mumbai
Nairobi Paris São Paulo Taipei Tokyo Toronto Warsaw
with associated companies in Ibadan

Oxford is a registered trade mark of Oxford University Press
in the UK and in certain other countries

ISSN 0017-3735
ISBN 0-19-852865-5

Typeset by Joshua Associates Ltd., Oxford
Printed in Great Britain
on acid-free paper by
Bell and Bain Ltd., Glasgow

PREFACE

Reception studies in Classics is a rapidly changing field. In preparing this contribution to the New Surveys series, I have been unashamedly didactic in trying to marry an outline of the current trends in the most interesting and influential areas of research to my arguments about the relationship between classical studies and broader cultural frameworks. In the ancient world, the texts discussed were not kept apart in ivory towers. Whether they were oral, written, built or performed they constituted a vibrant part of community culture and its often contested values and power struggles. Some aspects of reception studies suggest that this is beginning to happen once more. I hope that at least some of my suggestions will provoke further debate and that the discussion as a whole will encourage readers to look again at both the ancient and the modern texts.

At the request of the Series Editor almost all the references are to material published in English and I have also concentrated on those which are most easily accessible.

Academics and practitioners have, as always, been extremely generous in discussing their work with me, often in advance of publication or performance, and I thank them all. I am also extremely grateful to the students, friends and colleagues from various universities who have tried out material in seminars, contributed suggestions or criticized drafts. Special thanks are due to Carol Gillespie, David Fitzpatrick, Barbara Goff, Trish Thomas and Ian McAuslan, the Series Editor.

Lorna Hardwick,
Milton Keynes, October 2002

LIST OF ILLUSTRATIONS

1 Ajax carries the dead Achilles (both are named in the inscription). Detail from the handle of the François Vase (Black Figure Volute Krater from Chiusi, signed by Kleitias and Ergotimos). Florence 4209 (*ABV* 761).

2 Frank Brangwyn (1867–1956), *Study of a Canadian soldier supporting a wounded comrade.* Part of the design for a new parliamentary building in Winnipeg, entitled 'Canadian War Record'.
Photo: City of Birmingham Art Gallery.

3 Antony Sher as Domitian in the 2002 Royal Shakespeare Company production of *The Roman Actor* by Philip Massinger, directed by Gregory Doran.
Photo: Jonathan Dockar-Drysdale.

4 Italian terracotta by Antonio Canova (1757–1822). Maria Luisa Hapsburg, wife of Napoleon Buonaparte, who was Canova's patron, depicted as Concordia. *Concordia* was one of the concepts used in the public art and literature of the Roman Empire to sanction imperial rule. Concordia's companion piece depicts *Pax.*
Photo: National Gallery of Scotland, Edinburgh.

5 Greg Hicks as Teiresias in Sophocles' *Oedipus the King*, translated by Ranjit Bolt and directed by Peter Hall, National Theatre, 1996. Hicks' roles in Greek plays also include Orestes (*The Oresteia*, 1981), Agamemnon and Priam (*Tantalus* 2000/1) and Dionysus in *The Bacchai* (2002).
Photo: Alan Titmuss.

6 Maria Fierheller as Hecuba, holding Astyanax (in a bag of dust) in *Trojan Women*, adapted and directed by David Stuttard, Actors of Dionysus, 2002.
Photo: Dave Ashton.

7 *After Homer*, ODC Theatre Company, Edinburgh and the Opera House of Cairo 2002, directed by Elli Papakonstantinou. Stathis Mermigis in a music and movement sequence based on Aiolos' bag of winds and the storms endured by Odysseus (*Odyssey* X).
[This audiovisual performance/installation addresses the theme of 'return to home' through real time sound composition and processing, multi-screen video projections and layers of like multi-lingual text. Based on the ancient Greek text of the *Odyssey* and presented by a Greek-British company based both in London and Athens, the piece toured internationally in 2002 and received acclaimed reviews.]
Photo: Nikos Andritsakis.

CONTENTS

I. FROM THE CLASSICAL TRADITION TO RECEPTION STUDIES

On 30th January 1943, Adolf Hitler's close associate Goering made a radio broadcast to the beleaguered Sixth Army at Stalingrad on the eastern front. He compared the German army to the Spartan soldiers at Thermopylae in 480 BCE when they stood, fought and died to prevent the advance of the Persians ('the barbarians') into Greece. Goering's broadcast was not well received. The dispirited and starving listeners described it as 'our own Funeral Speech' and some officers joked ironically that 'the suicide of the Jews', besieged by the Roman army on the top of Masada in 73 or 74 CE was a more apt comparison.[1] This episode raises a host of questions about the reception of classical texts and ideas in later cultures. In this instance, not only was the classical allusion used as a model to sanction expectations of behaviour but further allusions were used as a counter-text to challenge the rhetoric of the high command.

At the turn of the twentieth and twenty-first centuries, a translation by Edwin Morgan of Racine's *Phèdre* into modern Scots was staged at the Royal Lyceum Theatre Edinburgh.[2] Morgan's translation into a Glaswegian-based Scots was part of a move to give status to the Scots language as part of the emerging classical theatre in Scotland. He also wanted to find out what it was about the play which would survive and transcend what he described as 'a jolt into an alien register'. The translation and the staging represented the latest point in a continuing commentary on the migration through successive languages and theatrical traditions of the story of Phaedra – Euripides' *Hippolytus*, Seneca's *Phaedra* and Racine's *Phèdre*. The function of reception studies is to analyse and compare the linguistic, theatrical and contextual aspects of this kind of migration.[3]

These examples demonstrate the extraordinary diversity in the range of classical receptions. Each has its own reception history and requires appropriate methods of investigation. Each yields insights into the texts

---

[1] The broadcast and reactions to it are described by Antony Beevor, *Stalingrad* (London, 1998), 380. Beevor comments drily, 'They did not realise how accurate they were. Hitler was indeed counting on a mass suicide, above all of senior officers.'

[2] Published text, E. Morgan, *Phaedra* (Manchester, 2000).

[3] See for example Amy Wygant, *Towards a Cultural Philology: Phèdre and the Construction of Racine* (Oxford, 1999).

and contexts of ancient works, their subsequent interpretation and their situation in the modern context of reception. The aim of this book is to engage with this rich cultural field by outlining the main features of current work in reception studies and discussing in more detail some of the most significant recent developments. This chapter sets out the conceptual and critical framework which the rest of the volume will use in the discussion of specific examples.

The increasing prominence of reception studies in relation to Greek and Roman texts, images, ideas and material culture is a fairly recent development. Although *Rezeptionsgeschichte* (reception history) or study of *Nachlebung* (afterlife) has been an important strand in German scholarship, its development in the international field and especially its adaptation in Anglophone scholarship has involved significant reshaping of the scope of reception studies and of the sources and methods used. In particular, the emergence of this specialism signals a move away from previous ways of looking at the relationship between ancient culture and its subsequent interpretation and adaptation. One strand in classical scholarship has been what was called 'the classical tradition'. This studied the transmission and dissemination of classical culture through the ages, usually with the emphasis on the influence of classical writers, artists and thinkers on subsequent intellectual movements and individual works.[4] In this context, the language which was used to describe this influence tended to include terms like 'legacy'. This rather implied that ancient culture was dead but might be retrieved and reapplied provided that one had the necessary learning. More recent research has tended to move away from the study of a linear progression of 'influence'.

The notion of some great chain of influence which linked great works of the Greeks and Romans to their counterparts in Renaissance, Enlightenment, Victorian and modern 'high culture' has fallen out of fashion. This is partly to be regretted since studies of transmission of texts and canon formulation and adaptation are valuable adjuncts to other aspects of classical study and help to explain how and why classical texts have been interpreted in particular times and contexts.

---

[4] Among outstanding works of this kind are G. Highet, *The Classical Tradition: Greek and Roman Influences on Western Literature* (Oxford, 1949); R.R. Bolgar, *The Classical Heritage and its Beneficiaries* (Cambridge, 1954); M.I. Finley (ed.), *The Legacy of Greece* (Oxford 1981); R. Jenkyns, *The Legacy of Rome: a New Appraisal* (Oxford, 1992). It is interesting to compare their scope and methods with a recent study such as T.P. Wiseman (ed.), *Classics in Progress: Essays on Ancient Greece and Rome* (Oxford, 2002), which contains chapters on 'Contemporary Poetry and Classics' (Oliver Taplin) and 'Socrates on trial in the USA' (Malcolm Schofield).

However, one good reason for the replacement of the methods of 'the classical tradition' as the sole means of studying classical texts through time is that such an approach was based on a rather narrow range of perspectives. Furthermore, it could carry an assumption, sometimes tacit sometimes explicit, that these works yielded a 'meaning' which was unproblematic, there to be grasped and to be applied in all kinds of situation far removed from the ancient one. Thus the associations of value carried with it were narrow and sometimes undervalued diversity, both within ancient culture and subsequently.

The diversity of ancient culture itself is now more widely recognized and interest has focused on ways in which some aspects were selected and used ('appropriated') in order to give value and status to subsequent cultures and societies and to inspire new creative work. This kind of study has proved valuable in that it has enabled people to distinguish more readily between the ancient texts, ideas and values and those of the societies that appropriated them. So, for example, we are less likely to simply confuse Greek and Roman cultural practices with those of the Victorians who filtered their appropriations of the ancient world into education, the arts and social values.[5] This increased sense of discrimination in examining the interfaces between cultures has had the further valuable effect of liberating the ancient texts for re-appropriation and reworking ('refiguration') by new generations of writers and artists. It is of course true that 'guilt by association' has sometimes remained a potent factor in causing rejection of the societies and values of Greeks and Romans as part of modern cultural studies. It can hardly be denied, for instance, that Athenian society in the fifth century BCE, a society which saw a flowering of the arts, was based on slavery of various kinds (in common with most of the ancient world and much of the modern) nor that the material improvements associated with Roman culture were disseminated as a result of the success of its imperial war machine. Appropriation of the practices, attitudes and values of Greek peasant society by the modern far right or of the public buildings, emblems and propaganda of the Romans by empire-builders and totalitarian régimes acts as an awful warning of the unlovely effects of uncritical adulation of any culture.[6] Such issues are of particular concern in reception studies,

[5] Particularly important in recent scholarship in this field are R. Jenkyns, *The Victorians and Ancient Greece* (Oxford, 1980); F.M. Turner, *The Greek Heritage in Victorian Britain* (New Haven, CT, 1981); G.W. Clarke (ed.), *Rediscovering Hellenism: the Hellenic Inheritance and the English Imagination* (Cambridge, 1989).

[6] For discussion of appropriation of Greek civic values by extremists in the USA see Page du Bois, *Trojan Horses: Saving the Classics from Conservatives* (New York and London, 2001). For

where the focus is on the two-way relationship between the source text or culture and the new work and receiving culture. Analysis of the principles and assumptions underlying selectivity and contextual comparisons between source and receiving conditions are vital tools.

It is important also to be aware that interest in reception of classical texts is not just a modern phenomenon. Greek and Roman poets, dramatists, philosophers, artists and architects were also engaged in this type of activity – refiguration of myth, meta-theatrical allusion, creation of dialogue with and critique of entrenched cultural practices and assumptions, selection and refashioning in the context of current concerns. Reception within antiquity is an important mediating factor between classical and modern cultures. Greek drama, for instance, did not cease in the fifth century BCE. There were important fourth-century and Hellenistic activities and the Romans, too, selected and adapted in order to create their own cultural traditions of comedy, of distinctive tragedies by Seneca and others, and of pantomime.[7]

Because reception is concerned with the relationship between ancient and modern texts and contexts, as well as with those separated by time within antiquity, it has implications for the critical analysis of both. It used sometimes to be said that reception studies only yield insights into the receiving society. Of course they do this, but they also focus critical attention back towards the ancient source and sometimes frame new questions or retrieve aspects of the source which have been marginalized or forgotten.[8] Reasons for such marginalizations are often significant. This means that reception studies have to be concerned with investigating the routes by which a text has moved and the cultural focus which shaped or filtered the ways in which the text was regarded.[9] Reception studies therefore participate in the continuous dialogue between the past and the present and also require some 'lateral' dialogue in which crossing boundaries of place or language or genre is as important as crossing those of time.

discussion of the institution of slavery in Greece and its effect on scholarship see most recently Paul Cartledge, 'Greek civilisation and slavery' in T.P. Wiseman (ed.), *Classics in Progress: Essays on Ancient Greece and Rome* (Oxford, 2002), 247–62.

[7] For discussion of this aspect see D. Wiles, *The Oxford Illustrated History of Theatre* (Oxford, 1995), ch. 2.

[8] See the discussion and references in L. Hardwick, 'Convergence and divergence in reading Homer' in C. Emlyn-Jones, L. Hardwick and J. Purkis (edd.), *Homer: Readings and Images* (London, 1992), 227–48.

[9] 'Text' is used in its broadest sense throughout this discussion to include oral sources, written documents and works of material culture such as buildings or sculpture. Each type of text of course makes particular demands in terms of description and analysis of its form and content.

Reception studies, therefore, are concerned not only with individual texts and their relationship with one another but also with the broader cultural processes which shape and make up those relationships. The discussions in this volume will be concerned with two main aspects of reception studies:

1. *The reception itself*

(i)   The artistic or intellectual processes involved in selecting, imitating or adapting ancient works – how the text was 'received' and 'refigured' by artist, writer or designer; how the later work relates to the source.
In relation to this it is necessary to consider

(ii) The relationship between this process and the contexts in which it takes place. These contexts may include: the receiver's knowledge of the source and how this knowledge was obtained; a writer's or artist's works as a whole; collaboration between writer/translator or director and designer and actor; the role of the patron or financier; the role of the audience/reader/public (both actual and imagined). In other words, factors outside the ancient source contribute to its reception and sometimes introduce new dimensions.

(iii) The purpose or function for which the new work or appro-priation of ideas or values is made – for instance, its use as an authority to legitimate something, or someone, in the present (whether political, artistic, social, or educational or cultural in the broadest sense).

2. *How the reception is described, analysed, evaluated*

No description is neutral and the forms, concepts and categories used by reception critics need clearly to indicate the extent to which they are using ancient categories to analyse and judge modern receptions. For example, discussion of a modern production of Greek drama would almost certainly consider how the chorus was represented and staged and whether masks were used. It might, but frequently does not, include assessment of the degree of equivalence to other ancient practices such as how the chorus was awarded and financed, i.e. the social and economic values underlying the staging of the play.

Equally, reception studies at all periods have been shaped by current

Fig. 1 Ajax carries the dead Achilles (both are named in the inscription). Detail from the handle of the François Vase (Black Figure Volute Krater from Chiusi, signed by Kleitias and Ergotimos). Florence 4209 (*ABV* 761).

conceptual and theoretical frameworks that shape and define 'knowledge'. Trends in modern literary and cultural theory, for instance, have stressed ambivalence and indeterminacy in the meaning attributed to texts, and disjunction and fissure in what might earlier have been seen as broader cultural certainties. For those reasons, reception of classical texts is playing an increasingly important part in studies of the cultural politics associated with change – for instance in the emancipation of Eastern Europe in the last part of the twentieth century and in post-colonial drama and literature. The appropriations and refiguring of classical texts in these contexts provides a yardstick of comparison between writing in independent and in colonized societies and the nature of the receptions is a significant indicator of cultural change.

In addition to the general influence of literary and cultural theory there are some theoretical approaches which impact directly on reception issues. Three have been particularly influential. In the 1960s

Fig. 2 Frank Brangwyn (1867–1956), *Study of a Canadian soldier supporting a wounded comrade*. Part of the design for a new parliamentary building in Winnipeg, entitled 'Canadian War Record'. Photo: City of Birmingham Art Gallery.

Hans Robert Jauss developed a theory of the 'aesthetics of reception' (*Rezeptions- ästhetik*). [10] This asserted that the historical character of an artwork could not be captured merely be describing it (as did the Formalists) or examining its production (as did the Marxists). Instead Jauss developed a theory of the interaction of production and reception. This involved dialogue between producer/artist and reader/audience/consumer. To frame this dialogue Jauss used the notion of a 'horizon of

[10] H.R. Jauss, *Towards an Aesthetic of Reception*, tr. T. Bahti (Minneapolis, 1982).

expectation'.[11] Jauss's adaptation of the concept focused on a horizon of experience of life and thus rooted the receiver's mind-set in his or her social and cultural context. This was what could be said to shape expectations and interpretations of texts.

A related theoretical response was that of Wolfgang Iser. Iser's main theoretical work appeared in the mid 1970s. Jauss's background was in literary history, Iser's is in English literature and his work focuses on reader-response as a trigger for the construction of meaning in literary texts (and by extension in drama, although comparable theoretical work on audience response is still lacking).[12] Iser's work covers the input to interpretation of a literary text by both the 'actual' reader and the 'implied' reader, that is the reader to whom the structure and language of the text speaks.

The third major theorist whose work has influenced reception studies is Hans-Georg Gadamer. His major work was published in the 1960s and 1970s.[13] Gadamer's main, although indirect, contribution to reception studies was his theory that the meaning to be attributed to a text is not 'essential', i.e. waiting to be drawn out, but constructed as part of the historical nature of understanding ('a fusion of horizons between past and present'). The implications for the study of classical texts are important since they suggest that the meaning attributed to an ancient text is shaped by the historical impact of its subsequent receptions. Even if one modifies Gadamer's theory to the weaker position that subsequent receptions have at least a contributory effect on the interpretation of ancient texts, this alone would justify a major scholarly role for the study of the histories of aesthetics of reception.

This possibility leads to a fourth theoretical approach which is sometimes used in reception analysis. This is the concept of 'critical distance' which uses the distance in time, place and culture that exists between ancient and modern versions of a text in order to enable the reader/spectator to move outside the limits of his or her own society and cultural horizons and thus to see these more clearly and more critically.

---

[11] This was based on the work of Karl Popper, the philosopher of science and Karl Mannheim, the sociologist and had been elaborated by Ernst Gombrich in *Art and Illusion* (Princeton, 1960). For discussion see Robert C. Holub, *Reception Theory: a Critical Introduction* (London, 1984).

[12] W. Iser, *The Act of Reading : a Theory of Aesthetic Response* (Baltimore and London, 1978). On drama and the audience see S. Bennett, *Theatre Audiences: a Theory of Production and Reception* (London and New York, 1990). On the Audience as potential 'translator' see L. Hardwick, 'Who owns the plays? Issues in the Translation and Performance of Greek Drama on the Modern Stage', *Eirene* 37 (2001), Special Edition *Theatralia*, 23–39.

[13] H-G. Gadamer, *Truth and Method*, first published 1960; the translators G. Barden and J. Cumming (New York, 1975) used the second edition (1965).

This concept is important both for envisaging the possibility of the individual or group enlarging horizons of expectation or even transforming them and for its potential when classical texts are used as critical devices for outwitting censors and enabling current social and political concerns to be addressed through the apparently neutral, 'distant' (and safe) medium of classical culture.

Towards a working vocabulary for reception studies

The vocabulary used in this study is centred round the central questions of how the reception in question and its context relate to the classical source and its context.

Acculturation	assimilation into a cultural context (through nurturing or education or domestication or sometimes by force)
Adaptation	a version of the source developed for a different purpose or insufficiently close to count as a translation
Analogue	a comparable aspect of source and reception
Appropriation	taking an ancient image or text and using it to sanction subsequent ideas or practices (explicitly or implicitly)
Authentic	close approximation to the supposed form and meaning of the source. At the opposite end of the spectrum from invention (i.e. a new work)
Correspondences	aspects of a new work which directly relate to a characteristic of the source
Dialogue	mutual relevance of source and receiving texts and contexts
Equivalent	fulfilling an analogous role in source and reception but not necessarily identical in form or content
Foreignization	translating or representing in such a way that *difference* between source and reception is emphasized
Hybrid	a fusion of material from classical and other cultures
Intervention	reworking the source to create a political, social or aesthetic critique of the receiving society
Migration	movement through time or across place; may involve dispersal and diaspora and acquisition of new characteristics

Refiguration	selecting and reworking material from a previous or contrasting tradition
Translation	literally from one language to another. Literal, close, free are words used to pin down the relationship to the source as are phrases like 'in the spirit rather than the letter'. Translation can also be used metaphorically as in 'translation to the stage' or 'translation across cultures'. Free translations sometimes merge into adaptations or versions
Transplant	to take a text or image into another context and allow it to develop
Version	a refiguration of a source (usually literary or dramatic) which is too free and selective to rank as a translation

The approach adopted in this study is not limited by any one of the theoretical positions outlined above, although it is informed by them all. My discussion is framed by these key assumptions:

(i) Receptions do in practice affect perceptions of and judgements about the ancient world and therefore need to be analysed.

(ii) Receptions within antiquity need to be considered within the same framework of enquiry as subsequent receptions so that the diversity of ancient culture is more fully recognized and the impact of ancient reception approaches on intervening interpretations is investigated.

(iii) Reception studies require us to look closely at the source text and context as well as at the receiving ones. This does not imply that the source is a yardstick of value but rather that a 'critical distance' between source and reception illuminates both. The traditional practices of classical philology have an important part to play in developing the broader cultural philology that reception studies needs.

(iv) The concept of cultural horizon (with its ancient analogue *paideia*) provides a useful but not constraining framework for reception studies. How cultural horizons, with their assumptions, expectations, aspirations and transformations, relate to classical material is a crucial area in modern reception studies which also have to take into account the impact of new technologies and art forms (such as film).

(v) Reception practice and its analysis reveals both commonalities and differences between ancient and modern. The shifting balance between commonalities and differences undermines the crudely polarized positions that classical texts either address universal and unchanging aspects of human nature or that they are remote and alien with nothing of value to offer to post-classical experience.

(vi) Reception of classical material is an index of cultural continuity and change and therefore has a value beyond its role in classical studies.

(vii) Reception is and always has been a field for the practice and study of contest about values and their relationship to knowledge and power.

The examples discussed in this volume are necessarily selective. Where possible I have focused on material which is widely available and to which readers can develop their own critical response. Art and architecture are mentioned only in passing as they would require a separate and extensively illustrated study. Similarly philosophy and historiography are only briefly discussed (with further suggestions in the Bibliography). Film gets a fuller discussion, partly because it presents issues of analysis and evaluation which are of particular interest in reception studies and partly because it represents a new aspect not only of classical receptions but also of the *paideia* in which they are embedded.

II. RECEPTION WITHIN ANTIQUITY

This chapter is in three sections. The first sets out the proposition that movements in ancient oral, written and material culture themselves involved reception and refiguration of material from inside and outside the Hellenic and Roman world. The second section looks at some aspects of these receptions and at the scholarly and critical tools which were developed in association with them and which have often set the parameters for subsequent investigation and evaluation. The third section identifies some important examples of how different aspects of reception within antiquity have contributed to the patterns of reception with which scholars and practitioners have engaged in subsequent periods. Overall, the model used is one which will be taken forward in later chapters of the book. It consists of an axis between reception as activity, as 'doing', 'making', 'responding' and 'creating' and reception as selecting, analysing and evaluating. The points of intersection are many but the more divergent areas of the model are also significant and may also contribute to dialogue between ancient and modern. Many critical terms and categories set out in the ancient world have fed into modern systems and in turn many aspects of modern practice, of reception 'activity', have prompted further analysis of cultural practices in the ancient world.

Cultural Analogues, Refigurations and Contests

It is an underlying contention of this study that reception within antiquity, as well as subsequently, was multi-faceted. It included diverse cultural practices, and the balance between borrowed, traditional and new perspectives in individual works of art and literature, in philosophy and historical writing and in broader cultural movements, is not only a subject of research and debate for study of the ancient world itself but also often informs studies of later receptions. The examples that follow illustrate this diversity.

Cultural paradigms and analogues

On the Great Sphinx Stela of Amenhotep II at Giza (New Kingdom eighteenth Dynasty, c.1400 BCE) a narrative passage exalts the achievements and reputation of the young king – 'he had no equal on the field of battle . . . there was not his like in this numerous army. Not one among them could draw his bow'.[1] The image of the bow as an instrument of moral and religious retribution is found also in the texts of the Hebrew Bible. For example in Psalm 21 –

For they intended evil against thee: they imagined a mischievous device which they are not able to perform.

Therefore, thou shalt make them turn their back, when thou shalt make ready thine arrows upon thy strings against the face of them.

Book XXI of Homer's *Odyssey* is often known as the book of the bow. The bow, which has a religious genealogy, becomes not only the symbol of Odysseus' wealth and power but also a test. The image of the bow has a varied cultural provenance. In the context of recent archaeological and anthropological study of the sea-borne cultural interaction which took place in the Eastern Mediterranean, Aegean, North Africa and the Near East from the sixteenth to the sixth centuries BCE the examples I have given suggest that in the *Odyssey* the specific poetic deployment of the image of the bow was informed and enriched by a network of cultural associations. These saw the bow as an emblem of physical prowess and military achievement, the epitome of craftsmanship, a divinely sanctioned instrument of vengeance and retribution, and a test of the qualities that heroic figures wished to be remembered by and have preserved for posterity. In this respect the poetic development of the *Odyssey* resonates with analogues from other cultural contexts which are oriental as well as Greek.[2]

---

[1] M. Lichtheim, *Ancient Egyptian Literature volume II: The New Kingdom* (Los Angeles and London, 1976), 39–43.

[2] See further L. Hardwick, 'Classical distances' in D. Sewart (ed.), *One World Many Voices vol. 1* (Milton Keynes, 1995), 283–6; S.P. Morris, *Daidalos and the Origins of Greek Arts* (Princeton, 1992); W. Burkert, *The Orientalising Revolution : Near Eastern Influence on Greek Culture – the early Archaic Age* (Cambridge, Mass. and London, 1992); M.L. West, *The East Face of Helicon : West Asiatic Elements in Greek Poetry and Myth* (Oxford, 1997); J.K. Davies, 'Greek History: a discipline in transformation' in T.P. Wiseman (ed.), *Classics in Progress: Essays on Ancient Greece and Rome* (Oxford, 2002), 225–46. Davies discusses 'a more realistic discourse which treats Greek and Eastern Mediterranean history as a continuum and thereby begins to dissolve the intrinsically racist distinction between 'Greek' and 'oriental', 235–6.

Refigurations

An aspect of refiguration which is important in both ancient and subsequent receptions is the adaptation of a legend or myth by the addition of new features. A good example is Aeschylus' attribution to Clytemnestra in *The Oresteia* of the active role in the killing of her husband Agamemnon on his return from Troy (especially *Agamemnon* 1372–98). In some other versions of the story her lover Aegisthus is the dominant figure and Aeschylus' handling of the myth shifts this part of the story as a *paradigm* for subsequent receptions.[3] Aeschylus' change intensifies the revenge cycle in the trilogy, sharpens the debate about the matricide (when Orestes avenges his father) and brings Clytemnestra to the fore as an active quasi-heroic figure in her own right. This has led to the emphasis in later receptions of the trilogy on the psychology of Clytemnestra and especially on her desire for revenge because of Agamemnon's sacrifice of their daughter Iphigenia in the hope of ensuring a fair wind for Troy (*Agamemnon* 1525–9). A number of modern productions have emphasized this aspect of the story, either by staging Euripides' *Iphigenia at Aulis* as a prelude to *The Oresteia* (as in Ariane Mnouchkine's production of *Les Atrides* (1992)) or by giving prominence to the chorus's account of the sacrifice, perhaps by including physical representation through mime or by the presence of Iphigenia as a ghost-like figure on the stage (as in Katie Mitchell's production of Ted Hughes's adaptation for the Royal National Theatre, 1999).

Such refigurations are not only found in ancient treatments of myth but also in ancient receptions of earlier texts from antiquity (for instance Virgil's reception of Homer). They indicate that, just as later receptions need to be considered in comparison with their source texts, so source texts need to be compared with the material which they themselves refigured and with other ancient treatments of the theme. This comparative perspective was used by ancient critics. For example, Dio of Prusa (late first century CE) included as his *Oration* 52 a short essay comparing the treatment of the story of Philoctetes by Aeschylus, Sophocles and Euripides, *Philoctetes in the Tragedians*.[4]

---

[3] For discussion of Aeschylus' relation to other ancient sources, see J. March, *The Creative Poet*, ICS *Bulletin* Supplement 49 (London, 1987), 79–118.

[4] For translation and commentary see D.A. Russell and M. Winterbottom (edd.), *Classical Literary Criticism* (Oxford, 1989), 188–91, 241.

Cultural Contests

These permeate both ancient and modern receptions and require attention to the socio-political contexts as well as to the texts themselves. A major area of debate, which has implications for later areas of reception as well as those within antiquity, is the reception of Greek culture by Rome, both in the Republic and the Empire and especially in the context of the Second Sophistic, the so-called revival of classical models in the early third century CE. Recent research in this field has explored the relationship between acquiescence and dissent, between assimilation and independence, between the discourses of cultural identity and political hegemony and between private reactions and public allegiance. Increasingly, the pattern which has emerged is one of ambivalence and contradiction with a particular sensitivity to the multi-vocal aspects of literary texts. As G.D.Woolf has summed up the general situation, 'Roman responses to Hellenism consisted of a complex and partly incoherent mixture of adoption, adaptation, imitation, rejection and prohibition, while the rhetorical poses repeatedly struck included assertions of admiration, of condemnation and of reconciliation'.[5] Such a summary can map literary and philosophical responses as well as social and political.[6] It also suggests a framework for examining later receptions of the texts which were themselves the product of contested receptions within antiquity.

Reception in antiquity; routes and tools

Of the mechanisms and channels for reception in antiquity the most important are transmission, translation and cultural focus. This last includes educational and religious environments, notions of *exempla* (images or lessons), and related concepts such as *imitatio* (imitation) and *aemulatio* (competition).[7]

---

[5] G. D. Woolf, 'Becoming Roman, staying Greek: culture, identity and the civilizing process in the Roman East' *PCPhS* 40 (1994), 116–43, quote at 120.

[6] For a summary of recent work in this area see T. Whitmarsh, *Greek Literature and the Roman Empire* (Cambridge, 2001), 1–5 and S. Goldhill (ed.), *Being Greek Under Rome* (Cambridge, 2001), esp. 1–25.

[7] Of course culture was 'spread', adapted and exchanged in the literal sense through material activities such as travel, seafaring, trade and warfare.

Transmission

Transmission is a complex cultural process which involves interplay between accidents of survival of monuments, artefacts and manuscripts and conscious selection and dissemination – whether of manuscripts or public and private styles of art. Transmission has been closely linked to the phenomenon of canon formation in which certain works survived in written form.[8] In a study of the process through which Athenian tragedy was transformed into an art form which was disseminated throughout the Greek-speaking world, translated and imitated by Roman dramatists, 'mutated into various types of balletic and operatic performance, and as a select corpus of classical texts helped to shape the educational system, and inform the culture of later antiquity', P.E. Easterling has shown that, despite the range of inscriptional and material evidence, in antiquity the history of performance was on its own insufficient to ensure the survival of complete tragedies in a form in which they could be transmitted from antiquity to later periods.[9]

The early evidence for 'canon' formation in Greek drama includes an official competition for revivals of fifth-century plays at the City Dionysia, which may indicate the emergence of a classical repertoire. Play texts from Greek tragedy after the fifth century BCE survive only in brief fragments and quotations, although study of New Comedy has been informed by papyrus finds. There appears to have been legislation in the fourth century BCE to prevent large-scale adaptation of texts by acting companies (see Plutarch's *Lycurgus*) but in other respects the transmission of a corpus of selected texts depended on the activities of scholars from the time of Aristotle to the Alexandrian researchers who collected, emended, classified and analysed texts.[10]

There had been a long-established tradition of libraries in the near east dating back to inscribed papyrus texts in the temple accounts of Abusir, c.2450 BCE. From the same period there survive statues of seated scribes. Most of the attested Egyptian and near-eastern collections were originally developed for administrative or religious needs. Papyrus or leather was used. Papyrus was the main material in the

---

[8] *Kanon* in Greek meant a measuring rod, standard or model. From the fourth century it was applied to New Testament books accepted as authoritative by the Christian church. Only later was it used to describe the most highly valued works in a particular cultural tradition.

[9] P.E. Easterling, 'From repertoire to canon' in P.E. Easterling (ed.), *The Cambridge Companion to Greek Tragedy* (Cambridge, 1997), 211–27, esp. 211, 224–7.

[10] See P.E. Easterling and B.M.W. Knox (edd.), *The Cambridge History of Classical Literature*, vol. 1 'Greek Literature', ch. 1 (Cambridge, 1985).

Greek and Roman worlds and is represented on Attic vases, apparently to depict poetry, from c.500 BCE, although Herodotus mentions that leather was used by the Ionians when papyrus was scarce (Herodotus 5.58).

Book production and trading is well attested in Athens from the late fifth and fourth centuries BCE and the oldest surviving specimens of literary papyrus rolls date from the second half of the fourth century. The development enabled Aristotle and his followers to collect books and establish libraries (Strabo 13.608). The Museum and the Library at Alexandria, founded by Ptolemy 1 Soter became a vital centre for scholarship and literary criticism which was influential in the transmission and broader reception of texts for many centuries, standardizing layout and format in ways which also grouped works by structure and theme, thus anticipating later genre categories. Alexandrian scholars also developed a system of commentary writing and this facilitated the survival of the selected works both in performance revivals and as material for future translators or imitators. The possibilities for interaction between the preservation of Greek tragedy texts, new performances and adaptations, and uses in education are shown in surviving fragments of school pupils' exercises, from quotations in anthologies and theatrical handbooks and from inscriptions attesting honours to later poets such as C. Julius Longianus (Aphrodisias in Asia Minor, second century CE).[11]

The theatrical influences on Roman culture enabled by the transmission of texts and the transplantation of associated images into other literary forms were considerable. Furthermore, it was the Romans who created the Codex, an important development in the shape of the book which led to cheaper pocket editions of literary texts by the first century CE (Martial 14.184–92). The innovation was exploited by the Christians for biblical texts from the early second century and in general greater availability and relative cheapness of books was a characteristic of the Roman world.

Christian attitudes to the religious and moral worth of some texts over others greatly influenced transmission patterns in late antiquity (when a new ecclesiastical class took over from the senatorial class as the most powerful commissioners and users) and subsequently into the medieval period, when Latin remained the official language of the Christian

---

[11] Text, translation and discussion in C. Roueché, *Performers and Partisans at Aphrodisias in the Roman and Late Roman Periods*, JRS Monograph 6 (London, 1993), 223–7.

Church in the West and monks took over the mantle of the Alexandrian Scribe. Seneca's tragedies were inimical to Christian theology and by the early Middle Ages were almost lost although his other works, of greater interest to moralists, prospered. The medieval circulation of the elegists Tibullus, Propertius and Catullus seems also to have been small. Physical destruction (by violence or the elements) played a part, but also crucial were selection and neglect. Some less favoured subjects and authors were preserved by transmission via Arab scholars through interaction with the Greek and Aramaic culture of the Eastern part of the Empire. This has been a particularly important channel for philosophical and scientific writings.[12] Patterns of selection, transmission and circulation were as important for the reception of texts in the ancient world as they are in the modern.[13]

Translation

Translation frameworks and trends are also an index to reception shared both by antiquity and by subsequent societies. In antiquity there were significant debates about the theory and practice of translation which are closely related to many of the debates in the recently developed modern discipline of translation studies. Furthermore, the cultural practices associated with translation in antiquity have equivalents across many of the diverse examples of modern receptions.

Various layers of bilingualism were present in antiquity. Herodotus knew only Greek and was dependent on Persian and Egyptian interpreters (2.125) but the Old Oligarch alleged that Athens in the late fifth century BCE contained a mixture of customs and languages 'from all the Greeks and barbarians' (2.8). It used to be thought that Greek was always used as the language of administration in the Hellenistic period but this assumption has been challenged, especially in respect of the Seleucid Empire for which the administration included Aramaic as well as Greek. In Ptolemaic Egypt, although Greek was the language of administration some individuals had double names, one Egyptian, one Greek, and there were scribes fluent in both demotic and Greek. As

---

[12] See further R. R. Bolgar, 'The Greek Legacy' in M.I. Finley (ed.), *The Legacy of Greece* (Oxford, 1981), 429–72, esp. 447–9 'Arab culture in the Middle Ages'; R.H. Rouse, 'The Transmission of the Texts' in R. Jenkyns (ed.), *The Legacy of Rome, a New Appraisal* (Oxford, 1992), 37–59 and L.D. Reynolds and N.G. Wilson, *Scribes and Scholars: a Guide to the Transmissions of Greek and Latin Literature* (Oxford, 2nd edition 1974).

[13] On ancient criteria and the importance of lists and excerpts, see P. Easterling, 'A taste for the classics' in T. P. Wiseman (ed.) (2002), 21–37.

Rome became hellenized, educated people increasingly became bi-lingual (from the first century BCE), although there were some reactions from figures as different as Cato and Juvenal, and Tiberius unsuccessfully discouraged the use of Greek in the Senate (Suetonius, *Tiberius* 71). However, there is a contrast between language used for cultural purposes and practices in the public service. The language of administration in the western part of the empire was Latin. This was also the language of law and the army. In the eastern part of the empire, Greek was used and official letters sent from Rome were usually translated into Greek first. Inscriptions such as the *Res Gestae* of Augustus were set up in Greek in the eastern part of the empire. Cornelius Gallus, made Prefect of Egypt by Octavian and also an elegiac poet, celebrated his suppression of rebellion, and alliance with Ethiopia, with a trilingual inscription (*CIL* 3 14147) accompanied by statues of himself. (Inevitably, he was recalled and ordered to commit suicide in 27/26 BCE.)

Translation and adaptation from Greek were important in the development of Latin literature. Livius Andronicus produced versions of Greek plays, a comedy and a tragedy, at the Ludi Romani of 240 BCE and his prestige was recognized by authorized permission for actors and stage poets to assemble in the Aventine temple of Minerva. His tragedies include titles such as *Achilles, Aegisthus, Ajax, Equos Troianus, Tereus.* There are also fragments of a translation of Homer's *Odyssey* into Saturnian verses (more usually used for epitaphs and commemorations). Cicero wrote disparagingly of the works (*Brutus* 71) although Horace referred to their use in schools (*Epist.* 2.1.69–71). Roman sensitivity to the relationship with Greek is underlined both by the efforts of Cicero and his circle to create a Graeco-Roman cultural awareness and by the view of Lucretius that Latin was limited in its scope compared with Greek (1.139).

The Romans categorized various translational approaches. Cicero, who himself produced translations of Greek texts as well as transplant-ing Greek ideas into Roman contexts, drew on his own experience to distinguish between translating word for word (*verbum pro verbo*) and translating in a way which communicated style and effect. Writing in 46 BCE, he discussed this in the context of his own translation of the speeches of the Attic orators Aeschines and Demosthenes – 'And I did not translate them as an interpreter but as an orator, keeping the same ideas and forms, or as one might say, the "figures" of thought, but in language which conforms to our ways. And in so doing, I did not hold it necessary to render word for word but I preserved the general style and force of the language'.[14] In analysing Cicero's statement the emphasis is usually put on his rejection of 'word for word' and his development of an interpretative strategy. However, it is equally important to note that he is discussing translation for performance. It must seem as if the orator's words were written in the language in which they were being spoken. This is an approach followed by many other translators for performance (and especially stage performance) up to the present day. An alternative strategy, to distance from the audience by archaizing or foreignizing would have a completely different impact which might have a purpose in theatre but in rhetoric would undermine the orator's prime purpose which is to persuade the audience that his words address their current situation.

Horace also rejected word-for-word translation, but for different reasons. In his *Ars Poetica* 133–4 (?20 BCE) he emphasized that translators should aim to produce work which was both aesthetically pleasing and had a creative impact in the receiving language. The Younger Pliny approached translation in a less creative way, stressing the utility of the exercise for stimulating critical linguistic awareness and precision as well as fluency (*Letters* 7.9.1). Cicero's approach was cited in a letter in 395 CE by St. Jerome as an authority for his own approach to translating the Septuagint (the Greek version of the Hebrew Bible) into Latin:

Now I not only admit but freely announce that in translating from the Greek – except of course in the case of the Holy Scripture, where even the syntax contains a mystery – I render not word for word, but sense for sense.[15]

Jerome elaborated on the idea of sense-for-sense translation by using the metaphor of the receiving language taking over the source language in the same way that a conqueror takes over a prisoner. However, it is important to note his caveat about the special demands of translating a sacred text. In that case both the meaning and syntax had to be proclaimed as sacrosanct since altering the sense could lead to a charge of heresy. (And of course, for those who regard classical texts as fixed in meaning, there are secular heresies which may be committed by too great a sensitivity to the receiving language.)

---

[14] Cicero, *De optimo genere oratorum* 14, tr. H.M. Hutbell (London and Cambridge, Mass., 1949).

[15] St. Jerome, *Epistolae* 57.5 tr. P. Carroll, in D. Robinson (ed.), *Western Translation Theory from Herodotus to Nietzsche* (Manchester, 1997).

Similar frameworks to translation have also been identified in the practices of the Arab translators (who were referred to above in the context of transmission). Greek scientific and philosophical texts were translated into Arabic in the Abbasid period (750–1250 CE), often with Syriac as an intermediary language. Two main translation methods have been identified.[16] The first method took an extremely literal approach in which each Greek word corresponded with an equivalent Arabic word and if no equivalent existed the Greek word was transplanted into Arabic. This method proved difficult and a second method developed. This was based on translating sense for sense, which aimed to communicate the sense of the Greek while not disrupting the Arabic. Scholars have pointed out that these practices had wider cultural effects in that concepts and thought systems also crossed into Arab culture and resulted in the development of Arab neologisms (rather than transliterations) while the translators also supplied extensive explanatory notes and commentaries.

This framework anticipates several fairly recent developments in translation practices in the languages of the British Isles. One is the increased use of glossed texts in reading ancient drama and poetry. These are texts in which key terms and concepts such as *pius* or *dikê* or *philia* or *aretê* are left in the original because they are thought to be untranslatable in that their semantic fields are not congruent with those of English equivalents. It is therefore a valuable heuristic activity for readers to consider their scope in each context of use.[17] Another development is the view of some translators of Greek tragedy into Scots that they are broadening and deepening the conceptual range of the various forms of the Scots language.[18] Finally, the stimulus experienced by the Arabic commentators finds an equivalence in the current initiatives towards developing new kinds of editions, translations and commentaries on classical texts to meet at the same time the basic linguistic and advanced intellectual needs of new generations of classics and classical studies students.[19]

In addition to distinguishing between word-for-word and sense-for-sense translations, Roman critics also developed a vocabulary for

---

[16] For further discussion, see M. Baker (ed.), *The Routledge Encyclopaedia of Translation Studies* (London and New York, 1997), 320–1.

[17] See further J. Parker, *Dialogic Education and the Problematics of Translation in Homer and Greek Tragedy* (Lampeter, Ontario and New York, 2000), esp. ch. 1.

[18] See below ch. 4, p. 63 with n. 28.

[19] See further D. Fitzpatrick, L. Hardwick, S. Ireland and D. Montserrat (edd.), *Old Wine, New Bottles: Texts for Classics in a Changed Learning Environment at University* (Milton Keynes, 2002).

describing other kinds of relationship between Greek texts and their Latin analogues. Key terms, each with slightly different philosophical, linguistic and metaphorical fields, included

vertere	to turn (often reflexive), to turn to account, to transform (also used by Livy in the sense of 'to rout')
mutare	to vary, change, shift and, significantly, to go into another country, to exchange. Can be used both transitively and intransitively and has a specific figurative use (*mutata verba*)
transferre	to carry over or across, to transfer, transport, convey or even to turn into. Cicero used this term to indicate translation into another language and also to indicate figurative or metaphorical use (*Att.* 6.2.3) while Quintilian used it to indicate analogues (2.15.21)
(Latine) exprimere	to mould, copy, express, portray (Cicero's usage covers to translate and to articulate)

The overlaps and differences between these usages are in some respects analogous to the debates today about the precise relationship to the source text of translations, versions and adaptations. However, to map a fuller range of interaction between source and new text an additional set of concepts is needed, indicating intersections between values and cultural practices. This range includes *imitatio, exemplum, aemulatio* and analysis of their use brings out the sometimes uneasy relationships between source and receiving cultures.

Cultural Forces

The cultural forces that shaped reception within antiquity were encapsulated in a number of key concepts that described various aspects of reception practices. These have also been influential in subsequent receptions, partly because of the cultural authority they acquired in the ancient world and partly because they describe aspects of the relationship between culture and power which scholars and critics have continued to apply to both ancient and modern receptions. I have selected five of these concepts because considered together they map the most important aspects of reception practices, within antiquity and subsequently, and because the relative crudity or relative refinement with which they have been used (in practice and in criticism) open up areas of reception that are discussed elsewhere in this study.

Exemplum is a Roman concept, originally used to refer to an image or object-lesson presenting a precedent from the past. Livy (59 BCE–17 CE) referred to these in his Preface to *Ab Urbe Condita Libri* (literally *Books from the Foundation of the City)*. This vast work covered Roman history from the origins of Rome to 9 BCE, originally in 142 books of which only 1–10 and 21–45 survive (and of these 41 and 43–5 have lacunae because of damage to the fifth-century manuscript which was the sole transmission for books 41–5). In his Preface Livy commented that 'the especially healthy and fruitful element of the study of history is this, that you contemplate object-lessons of every type of model set up on a conspicuous monument : from there you can choose for yourself and for your State what to imitate and what to avoid, if loathsome in its beginning and loathsome in its outcome'.[20] The conjunction of the precedent and the guide to moral behaviour is an influential feature of Roman attributes to the past. It was a constituent part of the desire for conformity to ancestral tradition which characterized values of the ruling class of the Roman Republic and was appropriated and adapted by the emperor Augustus and his successors in order that the authority of the Republican past should serve as a sanction for the imperial constitution and that they could claim to have 'restored the Republic'.

In a culture which values the receiving and adaptation of *exempla,* the patterns of choice of individuals or episodes as *exempla* have a particular significance. Livy himself focused in Book 1 of his history of Rome on the episode of the rape of Lucretia, which was supposed to have prompted the overthrow of the tyrannical dynasty of the Tarquins in 509 BCE when she was avenged by her brothers after her rape by Tarquinius Superbus. Livy's representation of this *exemplum* has several layers, including idealization of Lucretia as a Roman wife (she is surprised by her rapist while working at her loom and commits suicide to restore her reputation and, of course, that of her family). Livy's narrative also serves to equate the abuse of Lucretia with an attack on Rome and to lend support to the calls for the end to civil war and restoration of Republican values at the time at which he was writing in the 30s BCE.[21] The Lucretia episode was explored by other writers in

[20] Livy, Preface 9–10, translated and discussed by Susanna Morton Braund, *Latin Literature* (London and New York 2002), 21.
[21] See further, Braund (2002), 25–36.

antiquity (notably Ovid in *Fasti* ('*Roman Holidays*') 2.721–852) and also subsequently by both poets and artists (Shakespeare, Titian, Gentileschi, Tiepolo) and in opera, including Benjamin Britten's *The Rape of Lucretia*.[22]

The end of the monarchy in early Rome and the foundation of the Republic by Lucius Junius Brutus, who was elected as first consul, together with Lucretia's husband, also provided *exempla* for development by writers and artists. Thus Brutus became legendary for his strict sense of justice, which including putting to death his own sons when they were shown to be involved in the attempt to restore the Tarquins. This was discussed not only by Livy but also Plutarch (c.46–126 CE). The episode provided the inspiration for J-L. David's painting *The Lictors Returning to Brutus the Bodies of his Sons* which was in its final stages of completion for a Royal Commission in 1789. (David had already had a popular success with the exhibition of his *Oath of the Horatii* in 1785.) In this *exemplum* from the legends surrounding early Roman history of the seventh century BCE, three Roman brothers, the Horatii, fought for Rome in single combat against three Latin brothers, the Curiatii, in the struggle between Rome and Latium. David's addition of the return of the bodies to the family home, an element not mentioned by Livy or Plutarch, was thought to address the conflict between political duty and family allegiance which was so acute at times of political change.

The history of *exempla* demonstrates several recurrent features of reception history. Firstly, the *exempla* may be drawn from legend or remote history; this allows features to be adapted or added. There may be elements of the 'invention of tradition'. For instance Regulus, the Roman commander against Carthage in the First Punic War of the third century BCE, was heroized by Horace in *Odes* III.5 in which Regulus was represented as returning to Rome to negotiate peace after his capture by the Carthaginians, advising Rome to continue the war and then keeping his oath to return to Carthage where he faced torture and death.[23] Secondly, reception of *exempla* can involve a mixture of artistic, verbal and political elements. Thirdly, the cultural politics of the receiving context shape the reception which may contain an ambivalence or double-edged critique about contemporary matters or may be

---

[22] See further Ian Donaldson, *The Rape of Lucretia: a Myth and its Transformation* (Oxford 1982).

[23] Polybius does not refer to the episode and the story may have been invented to excuse the killing of prisoners from Carthage in Rome after Regulus' death (Diodorus Siculus 24.12.).

a blunt appropriation to sanction contemporary authority or values (see further chapter 3).

The use of *exempla* may carry a suggestion of the need to emulate. The ancient concept of *aemulatio* took this further and could imply competition. The concept has been most discussed in the context of the relationship between Greek and Roman literature where it represents an alternative to an emphasis on *imitatio* (imitation of Greek models). *Aemulatio* suggests a more culturally confident approach by Roman writers and artists who feel that they can take their places alongside those of Greece. The uneasy relationship between Greek culture and Roman conquest was most prominently addressed by Horace, who inverted the force of cultural and military power:

> Captured Greece took captive her rough conqueror
> And brought the arts to rustic Latium
> *(Epistles* 2.1.156–7)

However, although Greek literature remained as a yardstick for comparison, ancient authors certainly challenged by precept and in practice its claims to inevitable superiority. Quintilian referred directly to the merits of Latin literature and its challenge to the supremacy of the Greeks (*Training of the Orator* 10.1.93). Propertius commented in the 20s BCE, alluding to Virgil's development of the epic genre, 'give way, writers of Rome, give way, writers of Greece! Something greater than the *Iliad* is coming to birth' (2.34.65–6). The comment perhaps reflects Virgil's claim at the beginning of *Aeneid* 7 that he was 'setting about a greater work' as he moved onto the Iliadic battles of the second half of the poem. Philip Hardie has pointed out how Virgil's *imitatio* of Homer challenges the reader to compare and contrast source and imitation and how knowledge of the Homeric texts not only acts as a filter in reading the *Aeneid* but also enables the *Aeneid* to be read as a commentary on Homer. Hardie also shows how *exempla* are used competitively by characters within the *Aeneid* to enhance their status.[24] Poetic practice also involved re-workings and transplantations of poetic techniques into new contexts and is perhaps best described as a development of intertextuality rather than as simply *imitatio* or *aemulatio*. Examples include transplantation of images from Athenian tragedy into Roman epic (often mediated through allusions to Hellenistic writers). Servius, the fourth century CE scholar, noted this in his commentary on Virgil's

[24] See P. Hardie, *Virgil*, New Surveys in the Classics No. 28 (Oxford, 1998), 53–7.

Aeneid when he observed that *Aeneid* 4 draws on Apollonius' treatment of the Medea theme. Virgil also used Greek material on Medea even more creatively in his exploration of Dido's misery and rage when Aeneas leaves her.[25] Virgil also comments directly on his adaptation of the approaches and fields of reference of the Hellenistic poets at the beginning of his *Fourth Eclogue* –

> Sicilian Muses, grant me a slightly grander song,
> Not everyone delights in trees and lowly tamarisks;
> Let woods, if woods we sing, be worthy of a consul.
> *(Eclogue* 4. 1–3)

The allusion indicates that he is drawing on Theocritus, who came from Sicily and used Sicilian settings, but also that he is extending the private boundaries of the genre to include the public and the political.[26]

Thus it is clear that *exempla, imitatio,* and *aemulatio* are not self-contained categories. Even an apparent 'imitation' is not just an attempt at reproduction but in various ways involves transplantation and transformation. This may involve literary constructions which both use and challenge the excellence of the past. The representations and innovations involved are reflected in the debates about the concept of *mimêsis,* which covers both imitation and artistic representation of literature from the past. Ways in which these processes were performed in the ancient world reveal contests for cultural supremacy and shifts in what was thought to constitute 'Hellenism' and '*Romanitas*' together with a high degree of fluidity and overlap, especially in philosophy, literature and historiography.[27]

The fourth and fifth concepts which frame discussion of reception within antiquity are both highly contested terms. *Mimêsis* was a concept with which ancient literary criticism was directly concerned and the debates that ensued are both part of reception within antiquity and a shaping force in the later history of classical criticism and thus also in subsequent receptions. Indeed, much of the critical vocabulary and concepts used in modern literary criticism has been inherited and adapted from ancient critics. Of these the most influential have been Plato (especially *The Republic* Books 2, 3 and 10 and *Ion*), Aristotle *(Poetics)*, Horace *(The Art of Poetry)*, Longinus *(On the Sublime)* and

---

[25] See Virgil *Aeneid* 4. 522–32 and discussion in Braund (2002), 248–50.

[26] For further discussion, see Braund (2002), 254–7, and Hardie (1998), 5–10.

[27] For discussion of the politics of imitation and its relationship to *paideia*, with extensive references and bibliography, see Whitmarsh (2001), especially Part One, and Goldhill (2001), esp. 8–17.

Plutarch (*On the Study of Poetry*). However, from Homer, Hesiod and Pindar onwards poets self-reflexively commented on the nature of poetry, the function, fame and authority associated with it and on its power to affect the emotions and so potentially effect change.[28] These early discussions emphasized that poetry was a craft as well as the product of inspiration and accepted that it was part of the competitive ethos of Greek society.

The emergence of comedy as a theatrical form intensified allusion to poetic practice and competition and also saw the development of aesthetic criticism. The first known use of the term *mimêsis* occurs in Aristophanes' *Thesmophoriazusae* (411 BCE) where it is used to indicate cross-gender dramatic impersonation. Further debates about *mimêsis* are closely connected with those on the power of language and the moral standing of poetry. The Sophists, especially Gorgias, discussed the power of poetic language. His rhetorical display oration *Encomium of Helen* examined the effect of speech on the mind, likening it to that of drugs on the body – sometimes beneficial, sometimes harmful. Gorgias' description of the impact of poetry on the emotions anticipated Plato's analysis of the dangerous effect of poetry and drama on audiences and also raised issues about the creation of pity and fear which were later taken up by Aristotle.

From the late sixth century BCE poetry was already under attack from philosophers and moralists; for example, the Ionian Xenophanes criticized poetry on the grounds that Homer and Hesiod attributed to the gods 'all things that bring shame and reproach to men: theft, adultery and deceit' (fragment B11). Critics also drew on the capacity of poetry to deceive – a tradition based partly on the fluidity of myth and partly on the discussion of deception in poets from Hesiod onwards, some of which anticipates notions of fiction as a genre. A related development to the exploration of poetry's capacity to deceive was the concept of allegory, which started as a defence of poetry's fluidity of meaning and developed into a systematic critical approach which, especially in the context of Stoic and Neoplatonist thought, could be aligned with a sense of moral and social insight.

---

[28] For discussion of this aspect with examples see P. Murray, introduction to P. Murray and T.S. Dorsch (edd.), *Classical Literary Criticism* (London, 2000). Translated extracts from Plato, Aristotle, Horace and Longinus are included in Murray, together with specialist bibliography and chronological tables of authors and events. There is a slightly wider selection, with explanatory notes, also including Horace's *A Letter to Augustus*, Tacitus' *Dialogue on Orators*, Dio of Prusa's *Philoctetes in the Tragedians* and Plutarch's *On the Study of Poetry* in D.A. Russell and M. Winterbottom (edd.), *Classical Literary Criticism* (Oxford, 1998).

In contrast, Plato's critique of poetry was based on its alleged failure to lead to worthwhile knowledge. He argued that poetry encouraged hearers to emulate the degrading actions and emotions which it purported to represent and (somewhat paradoxically) that such representations were in themselves a sham. Since poets and dramatists had such contempt for truth he wished to have them excluded from his ideal state. Critics have commented on the paradox that Plato himself was a highly poetic and theatrical writer and have speculated that his fear was based on the fact that these were popular art forms permeating Greek education and including all sections of society in their transmission of shared cultural horizons and values.[29] Plato's discussion of *mimêsis* initially centres on the way in which the poet or performer adopts the guise of a character and almost becomes that person, thus acting as a role-model for the audience. Subsequently, Plato extended the scope of his critique to other art forms, focusing on the way in which images and representations are unsubstantiated reflections of objects and have no true existence. This emphasis on triviality rather detracts from his alternative view of *mimêsis* as influential and potentially dangerous and this ambivalence has been reflected in a wide variety of responses, including a defence of poetry by the Neoplatonist Plotinus (third century CE) who argued that the poet can improve on the imperfections of nature.

The most influential work of literary criticism from the ancient world is Aristotle's *Poetics*. In contrast to Plato's stress on the inspired and the irrational, Aristotle concentrates on the rational principles underlying the poetic craft. His treatment of *mimêsis* stresses that the poet is a maker of likenesses, refashioning rather than copying. So, for example, the tragic poet would represent what might happen, rather than communicating the reality of what did happen, which would be the task of the historian. The poets' reality is, according to Aristotle, the reality of the imagination, although it must be plausible.[30] Aristotle discusses epic briefly; a section on comedy is lost and the bulk of the *Poetics* focuses on tragedy, with special attention to formal elements and conventions and on the effects on the spectators. His discussion of tragedy's association with the emotions of pity and fear and their catharsis (or healing) has been endlessly debated, sometimes as a precursor of psychoanalytical theory and sometimes as an attempt to depoliticize and neutralize the effects of theatre.

---

[29] For discussion, see Murray (2000), xxiii–ix.
[30] See Murray (2000), xxxii for discussion.

Aristotle was writing a century after the main developments in tragedy and in relation to these and in his response to the writing of Plato his work is itself a reception text. It lacked critical influence in antiquity but subsequently has played a major part in setting the conceptual framework for discussion and evaluation of tragedy. After its rediscovery by Italian humanists in the sixteenth century, Aristotle's *Poetics* was disseminated throughout Europe, where it was particularly influential in seventeenth-century French classical theatre. Even in the twentieth century, Aristotle's categories of discussion were often projected back on to Athenian tragedy as though the *Poetics* was a work of contemporary analysis rather than a reception which drew on several strands of cultural history.[31]

Paideia

This was and is a controversial concept. It can imply not only a process of acculturation and education but also access from this to a prized and sometimes exclusive body of texts, artworks and values. It thus draws on the routes of transmission and translation and is framed by the key concepts of description and evaluation which have been summarized above. Its status as the locus of Greek cultural identity provided a field for contest both within Hellenic culture and in its interactions with the Roman. From at least the fifth century BCE the forms and content of education had a definitive role in constituting what it was to be Greek and those who sought cultural hegemony also sought to appropriate *paideia* as a sanctioning force. Thus Pericles was represented by Thucydides in the Funeral Speech as putting forward Athens as an 'education' for Greece (Thucydides 2.41.1) in a context which exploited the language of education to present democratic Athenianism as the equivalent of Hellenism. The anti-democrat Plato needed to revise the concept for his ideal state and in the fourth century BCE Isocrates, writing for a more concrete situation, used Athenianism and its power as the basis for opening up Hellenism to élites who shared in its education and culture, rather than necessarily being Greek by descent (*Panegyricus* 50). Isocrates used Hellenism as a cultural sanction for a pan-Hellenic alliance to conquer the 'barbarians' of the East. Later the notion was further modified by the Alexandrians who

---

[31] See further S. Halliwell, 'Aristotle's *Poetics*' in G.A. Kennedy (ed.), *The Cambridge History of Classical Literary Criticism*, vol. 1 (Cambridge, 1989), 149–83.

presented themselves as 'educators of all the world, of both Greeks and barbarians'.[32]

However, in Rome's progressive conquest of the Greek world, *paideia* could no longer be seen only as a defining quality of Hellenism. In the values of the Roman Republic Greece was seen not only as a source of culture and learning but also of luxury, trickery and military weakness.[33] In contrast Rome's traditional virtues were, if rustic and uncultured as Horace observed, at least the source of rectitude and military success. Virgil overcame Horace's queasiness and in *Aeneid* 6, lines 847–53, Anchises, in an epilogue to the Parade of Heroes, elevated Roman achievements to equal status, telling them to practise the arts of empire, just war, and the maintenance of law and order and to leave excellence in sculpture and oratory to others (i.e. Greeks). In an analogous move Cicero, an apparent promoter of Greek learning, stressed the need to use Greek culture to serve the ambitions of the Roman élite (*Tusculan Disputations* 1.1–3).[34] This imperative underlay his transplantations of Greek philosophy into Roman political contexts (as in *De Officiis*). The association of appropriation of Greek *paideia* with political shifts was exemplified when after the end of Domitian's régime (in 96 CE) Trajan used Greek associations to signal the change from Domitian's tyranny, which had been characterized by rejection and exile of philosophers. The cultural shift was taken further by Trajan's successors Hadrian and Marcus Aurelius.

The contested field of *paideia* within antiquity in some respects serves as an analogue for contests in subsequent receptions. In his discussion of the Second Sophistic, Simon Goldhill has pointed out that apparent nostalgia for the classical past was 'also veined with a complex dynamic of attraction and rupture, affiliation and dismissal. The question of whose past is to count and the ambivalence, redefinition and desire which inform such historicising pictures, mark such genealogies as the sites of contest as much as tradition'.[35] Struggles over the provenance of *paideia* and its values and political associations (from democratic to oligarchic to imperial), awareness of its potential for

---

[32] *FHG* 246.1 Andron = Athen.*Deipn.*184b. For further discussion and bibliography, see Whitmarsh (2001), 7–9.

[33] For the variety of forms taken by these stereotypes see the precepts of the Elder Cato, the rejection of Greek philosophy in the second century BCE and in Imperial literature Juvenal's *Satires*, especially *Satire* 3.

[34] For further discussion see S. Swain, *Hellenism and Empire: Language, Classicism and Power in the Greek World AD50–250* (Oxford, 1996) and Whitmarsh (2001), 12–20.

[35] Goldhill (2001), 8.

facilitating assimilation across cultures and successive shifts in the status of the aesthetic and educational practices from which it was constituted prefigure the struggles for selective appropriation, accretion and redefinition of classical culture which recur in the debates surrounding modern receptions. It is these debates which are the concern of the chapters which follow.

III. CHALLENGING STEREOTYPES – THE CONTEXTS OF RECEPTION

This chapter broadens the basis of the discussion in three respects. Firstly, the discussion will include examples which show how the history of reception of ancient texts and ideas is intermingled with and to some extent shaped by the artistic forms and cultural politics of receiving traditions. This means that in looking at examples of modern reception it is necessary to consider the routes through which the ancient text or idea itself has passed and the way in which subsequent cultural assumptions filter modern representations. Secondly, I have deliberately chosen examples which engage with the claim that the ancient world provides models, either in the sense of examples of how human beings might behave or, more subtly, ways in which Greek or Roman history or culture has been presented as a base from which subsequent generations might analyse and critique not just the ancient world, but also their own. In this aspect of the discussion I shall challenge the notion, put forward by a number of critics and most recently fostered by Page du Bois,[1] that those looking to the ancient world as a source of insight, whether artistic, moral or political, are necessarily conservatives. Thirdly, in pursuing this argument I shall also begin to scrutinize and revise any easy assumptions that may linger concerning underlying differences in the ways in which it is possible to characterize Greek and Roman material and its reception or about restrictions in the variety and potential of either. The focus here will be on Roman ideas and texts. The next chapter will concentrate on Greek examples.

'The Roman Actor'

All the key issues that I summarized above came together in the summer 2002 production, by the Royal Shakespeare Company at Stratford-upon-Avon, of Philip Massinger's tragedy *The Roman Actor*. The performance was part of a season devoted to the revival, by an ensemble company of twenty-eight actors, of five little-known and seldom staged sixteenth- and seventeenth-century plays.[2]

---

[1] In *Trojan Horses: Saving the Classics from Conservatives* (New York and London, 2001).

[2] The others were: William Shakespeare, *Edward III*; Ben Jonson, John Marston and George Chapman, *Eastward Ho!*; John Fletcher, *The Island Princess*; John Marston, *The Malcontent*.

In his introduction to the published play text[3] the season's artistic director, Gregory Doran, commented on the affinities between the public stages of the Rose and the Globe and that developed 400 years later at the Swan Theatre, 'The stages of the Rose and the Globe needed no scenery, that would be conjured by words, words spoken by the actor standing in the centre of a circle of ears. The Swan Theatre in Stratford reproduces just such a relationship between actor and audience: vital, immediate and dangerous' (p. viii).

In 1626 when the play was written, Philip Massinger was the chief playwright for the King's Men, his predecessors being Fletcher and Shakespeare. The company ran both the Globe Theatre in Southwark and the Blackfriars in the City. The play is one of several in the early seventeenth century that represent the history of Rome in the early Empire. Ben Jonson's tragedy *Sejanus* (1603) explored the machinations between the emperor Tiberius, his entourage and those opposed to the principate. Other plays dealt with more salacious themes (anon., *Tragedy of Nero*, ?1624; Thomas May, *Julia Agrippina*, 1628; Nathaniel Richards, *Messalina*, ?1635). The plays had in common the use of Tacitus as a source, and especially his treatment of the use and abuse of power and the role of the emperor. In his introduction to the play text, Martin Butler points out (p. xi) that Machiavelli's *Il Principe* (*The Prince*, 1513) was not yet translated into English and that mediation of the intrigues of statecraft via Tacitus' analysis of the early Empire led to an interest in Rome which provided an outlet for contemporary fears and concerns. Indeed, the rhetoric associated with the coronation of James I and VI had likened the king to a new Augustus who would both bring peace and secure lost empires.

James's successor Charles I was addicted to court entertainments which featured classical scenes in which he could dance the role of a Roman emperor entering the city in triumph. The attraction for him of this theme is proved by his purchase in 1628 of Andrea Mantegna's *Triumphs of Caesar* (eight huge paintings which are now part of the Hampton Court art collection, described in Butler, p. xi). It would perhaps be attributing to Massinger an excessive (and courageous) satirical zeal if one were to claim that his depiction in Act 1 scene 4 of *The Roman Actor* of Domitian entering Rome in triumph ('as we now touch the height of human glory, riding in triumph to the Capitol') actually alludes to Charles I's dancing fantasia. Some in the audience

---

[3] Philip Massinger, *The Roman Actor* (London, 2002), with introduction by Martin Butler.

might have made the connection (although few could have foreseen the eventual closure to the analogy when Charles, like Domitian, was killed because of his abuse of power). More important is the way in which the content and structure of the play examines the cultural and moral role of theatre and thus, in conjunction with the examination of the emperor's exercise of power, comments on issues which resonated with the contemporary situation.

The modern revival gave similar opportunities to the company and the audience. In the 2002 Swan Theatre production, directed by Sean Holmes, Antony Sher played the part of Domitian. His appearance was described by one reviewer as 'a shaven-headed biker/bouncer type'.[4] However, a better analogy in both appearance and behaviour would be with Mussolini. In addition to the theatricality of fascism, its bureaucracy was captured in Domitian's compulsive recording of murders in a black notebook.

The stage set was minimalist, just three pillars of which the central allowed Domitian to tower in almost divine triumph over the obsequious senate. In a situation where this 'parliament' (like that of Massinger's time) hardly met, senators who dissented were cruelly done to death. Junius Rusticus and Palphurius Sura were representatives of the 'old Romans' whose adherence to the values of the ruling class of the Roman Republic was mingled with inclinations towards Stoicism and opposition to the excesses of the new imperial order from Tiberius onwards but especially in relation to Nero and to Domitian. These emperors appear to have regarded Stoicism as an ideology of opposition. Massinger's play specifically alludes to the case of Thrasea Paetus, who was accused of giving public expression to criticisms of the emperor Nero by refusing to participate in public affairs and was eventually forced to commit suicide.[5] In *The Roman Actor*, as Rusticus is being violently tortured and tormented on-stage by Domitian he retorts:

> To guilty men
> It may bring terror; not to us, that know
> What 'tis to die, well taught by his example
> For whom we suffer. In my thoughts I see
> The substance of that pure untainted soul
> Of Thrasea our master, made a star,

---

[4] Julie Chamberlain, *Coventry Evening Telegraph*, 1st June 2002, 11.
[5] Tacitus, *Annals*, 16.21–35. As Tacitus put it, 'Thrasea's independence made others less servile', *Annals* 14.48.

Fig. 3 Antony Sher as Domitian in the 2002 Royal Shakespeare Company production of *The Roman Actor* by Philip Massinger, directed by Gregory Doran. Photo: Jonathan Dockar-Drysdale.

> That with melodious harmony invites us
> (Leaving this dunghill Rome, made hell by thee)
> To trace his heavenly steps.
>
> (Act 3, Scene 2)

However, another major theme of Massinger's play subverts the notion that an easy opposition between Republican virtue and Imperial excess is being portrayed in order to provide an example to all. The relationship of theatre to critique is undermined through the experiences of Paris, represented by Massinger as a tragedian.[6] At the beginning of the play there is a debate about the ethical value of drama which Paris cites in his defence against a charge of treason. According to this argument, spectators at a play are inspired to emulate virtue and reform vice. Referring to the moral stance of philosophers Paris claims:

[6] The historically attested Paris was a pantomime dancer, referred to by Juvenal in *Satire* 7.82–7 and executed in 83 CE for a supposed liaison with the emperor's wife. Another *pantomimus* of the same name was executed by Nero in 67 CE because of Nero's jealousy over dancing prowess (Suetonius, *Nero*, 54.1). The name 'Paris' therefore seems to have assumed generic associations of rivalry with the emperor.

> Or if desire of honour was the base
> On which the building of the Roman empire
> Was rais'd up to this height; if to inflame
> The noble youth with an ambitious heat
> T'endure the frosts of danger may deserve
> Reward or favour from the commonwealth,
> Actors may put in for as large a share
> As all the sects of the philosophers.
> They with cold precepts (perhaps seldom read)
> Deliver what an honourable thing
> The active virtue is. But does that fire
> The blood, or swell the vein's with emulation
> To be both good and great, equal to that
> Which is presented in our theatres?
> Let a good actor in a lofty scene
> Show great Alcides honoured in the sweat
> Of his twelve labours . . .
> . . . All that have any spark of Roman in them,
> The slothful arts laid by, content to be
> Like those they see presented.
>
>   (Act 1, Scene 3)

The tragedy was revived in 1690–92 and also in the eighteenth century. In the nineteenth century Paris' oration was sometimes performed on its own, an expression perhaps of the Romantic view that great art transforms. However, in Massinger's play his claims are found wanting. Paris performs at court and his first play, a satire on greed, fails to persuade the spectators to recognize themselves, let alone reform. The second play inspires Domitian's mistress to fall in love with Paris and in the third he is killed by Domitian who takes the role of avenger, a performative allusion to the belief that some Roman emperors killed condemned criminals on stage (or in the arena). So, as Butler puts it, 'this device allows him [Massinger] to put a question mark over the drama's immunity to the excess that characterises Domitian's Rome' (p. xii). Put more strongly, the powers of theatre itself could be said to be corrupting and, in a moral sense, illusory (as critics from Plato to the Puritans alleged). Massinger's reworking of Tacitean perspectives on the power intrigues of the early Roman empire in the context of the cultural and political debates surrounding the Stuart dynasty, and the modern revival, with its allusion not only to fascism but to the broader association of tyranny with theatricality, are subtle in separating the notion of 'playing' from political and moral didacticism. Yet there does remain in the play the implication that the qualities associated with the Roman Republic were recognized as morally virtuous and those associated with the imperial regimes were abusive, and corrupt. Further examples, however, indicate that these stereotypes, too, can be questioned.

Spartacus – constructing and appropriating a legend

The representation of the figure of Spartacus in modern film and fiction provides a map, not just of cultural politics in relation to particular art forms but also of a wider contest for control of iconic figures from the past, either to provide reference points or to have exemplary status in modern ideological struggles. Underlying the representations of Spartacus there are also differences in viewpoint between historians of the ancient world and those cultural historians who focus on reception. This is not merely a question of disagreement about the degree of significance of Spartacus as a historical figure in the context of the Roman slave wars (important though that is) or even about the relationship between individuals and broader trends in history, but more subtly about the relationship between the ancient evidence for the life of one man and the ways in which it has subsequently been refigured, both artistically and politically. In that sense the Spartacus debate is emblematic of many of the problems which are involved in reception studies.

In his book *The Ragman's Son: an Autobiography*[7] the Hollywood film actor and producer Kirk Douglas included a chapter 'The Wars of Spartacus' in which he wrote 'Spartacus was a real man, but if you look him up in the history books, you find only a short paragraph about him. I was intrigued with the story of Spartacus the slave, dreaming of the death of slavery' (p. 304). The last part of the quotation was used at the beginning of the 1980 film *Spartacus*. As Brent D. Shaw points out in his discussion of the passage, Douglas was anachronistically running together the ancient dream of escape from slavery with the modern aspiration of perpetual abolition.[8]

The slave uprising led by Spartacus in 73 BCE was in fact the third and last of a series of rebellions against Roman enslavement which took place between the middle 130s and the late 70s BCE. The first two had developed on the island of Sicily, which had been the first province of

---

[7] K. Douglas, *The Ragman's Son: an Autobiography* (New York, 1988).
[8] Brent D. Shaw, *Spartacus and the Slave Wars: a Brief History with Documents* (Boston and New York, 2001), 28.

the embryonic Roman empire.[9] Each of the first two slave rebellions was led by inspirational commanders. The third slave war was distinguished by the fact that it was waged in the south of Italy and not overseas. Spartacus was not the initial leader but emerged as the major figure. He was a Thracian and is thought to have been captured and sent to Italy to be sold as a slave. A significant feature of the form of slavery associated with Rome was that slaves were imported in large numbers by the conquering power and used to support and transform agriculture and other aspects of the economy.[10] Furthermore, in southern Italy and Sicily agricultural requirements meant that slaves were used as *pastores* (herdsmen). They had to be able to move around with the herds and thus were not housed in barracks as were the agricultural labourers on the lands producing crops (*latifundia*). Furthermore, the *pastores* had to be armed in order to protect the herds and flocks. So the *pastores* in Sicily and southern Italy were potentially a threat to the Roman system.

However, in the case of the third slave war, the leaders were not herdsmen but *gladiatores*, who had been trained to kill for entertainment. An inscription in Oscan on a wall-fresco from Pompeii gives the name Spartacus to a mounted gladiator, and since the date is probably 100–70 BCE identification with the leading participant in the slave revolt has been suggested. The historian Appian, writing two centuries after the events, records that 'Spartacus, a Thracian whom the Romans had imprisoned and then sold to be trained as a gladiator, had once fought as a soldier of the Roman army . . . persuaded about seventy of the enslaved men to risk a break for freedom . . . many fugitive slaves and even some free men from the surrounding countryside came to this place to join Spartacus . . . Since Spartacus divided the profits of his raiding into equal shares, he soon attracted a very large number of followers'.[11]

There is also important evidence, nearer in time and citing Spartacus by name, in Sallust, *Histories* Books 3 and 4, although much of it is fragmentary, and there are mentions in Livy and Plutarch. Appian attributes the success of Spartacus to good organization and management of resources. Only after three years did a Roman army under

---

[9] i.e. empire in that it had control of territory overseas although this was acquired while internally Rome still had a Republican constitution The term Empire should be reserved for the imperial constitution initiated by Augustus in the settlements of the late first century BCE.

[10] This feature of slavery is different from that developed later on from the sixteenth century by the European colonial powers. In that case slaves were transported to develop production in overseas territories: Shaw (2001), 8.

[11] Appian, *Roman History: the Civil Wars*, 1.14.116–21.

Crassus (who was vying with Pompey for victory against the rebels) gain victory in what Appian describes as 'a protracted battle of epic proportions'. Spartacus was killed and the rest of his army died in battle or were crucified by Crassus along the Appian Way. The number implies a crucified slave every 35–40 yards from Capua to Rome, a distance of 125 miles.[12] The devotion of this amount of attention to a slave is unusual in ancient sources and some historians have suggested that even at this stage the image of Spartacus was attracting its own 'mythology' and that two different traditions were emerging – that of Spartacus as of servile status and crucified by Roman power and that of Spartacus as a brave and skilled leader.

Modern appropriations of Spartacus have mostly followed the latter image but sometimes with variations that suggest the corrupting effects of power, even when nobly won. The best-known representation of Spartacus is in the 1960 film starring Kirk Douglas and directed by Stanley Kubrick. In this film Laurence Olivier played Crassus and it also featured Charles Laughton, Peter Ustinov, Tony Curtis and Jean Simmons (who supplied the love interest as Spartacus' wife Varinia, whose name is unsurprisingly not attested from antiquity). The film was rather loosely based on the best-selling novel *Spartacus* by Howard Fast.[13] Fast was thought to have been 'inspired' to write the book by his opposition to the McCarthy movement in the United States in the late 1940s and 1950s. Joseph McCarthy, a senator, led a movement to suppress any group, individual or art-work which was thought to be left-wing. He operated through the Un-American Activities Committee of the US Senate.[14] As a result Fast, who had been imprisoned for communist sympathies, was blacklisted by publishers and had to self-publish the novel. In this sense the 1960 film became a way of refighting the battles against McCarthyism (since its controls over the film industry had by that time eased).

There is, however, a long history underlying Fast's decision to pursue his fight for justice by using the image of Spartacus. From the 1760s the figure of Spartacus had been used by historians and philosophers,

---

[12] Towards the end of World War II when Soviet troops were moving towards Germany, the Red Army authorities exhumed the bodies of 65,000 Jews killed by the Nazis in Eastern Europe and displayed the bodies every 200 metres along the roads most used by troops with signs which read 'Look how the Germans treat Soviet citizens'. Source Anthony Beevor, *Berlin: the Downfall, 1945* (London, 2002), 169.

[13] H. Fast, *Spartacus* (New York, 1951), with further editions 1958, 1960, 1997.

[14] One of the effects of McCarthyism was the 'exile' to Britain of the ancient historian M.I. Finley.

especially in contexts discussing the validity of armed resistance to oppression. In a letter of 1769 Voltaire described the slave war led by Spartacus as a war which was just, 'indeed the only just war in history'.[15] This perhaps reflected the impact of anti-tyrannical literature such as Bernard Saurin's *Spartacus: a Tragedy in Five Acts*, performed at the Théâtre Français in 1760 as well as the academic studies by Charles de Brosses (presented as part of a history of the Roman Republic to the Academy of Inscriptions in Paris in May 1768) and Jean Lévesque de Burigny who published a work on the condition of Roman slaves in 1766–7. Perhaps the interest of French writers was stimulated by the incidence of slave rebellions in the overseas territories of the European colonial powers (for example the rebellion led by Boukman and Toussaint L'Ouverture in Haiti). Certainly at this time interest in Spartacus was not antiquarian but reflected contemporary commitment to freedom and liberty.[16]

A century after Voltaire Karl Marx identified Spartacus as one of his heroes, having read about him in Appian.[17] Marx's informed analysis was in its turn refigured in the twentieth century by Stalinists who likened the Roman slave rebellions to the French and Russian revolutions. Left wingers in Germany protested against the First World War and the economic situation in pamphlets bearing the signature 'Spartakus'. The movement led by Karl Liebknecht and Rosa Luxemburg was called the 'Spartakusbund' and after their assassination in 1919 the image of Spartacus attained iconic status. However, disillusionment with the evils of Stalinism also led to revisionist re-assessments of the Spartacus image. In his novel *The Gladiators*[18] Arthur Koestler transformed the myth into a study of a revolutionary movement which lost its noble ideals and descended into cruelty and tyranny – a Roman equivalent perhaps to George Orwell's *Animal Farm* (1954), in which liberation and subsequent descent into oppression is presented through the struggles of animals.

Reception of the Spartacus image in Italy took a somewhat different

---

[15] Voltaire, *Oeuvres* 53, volume 9 of *Correspondance générale*, 461–3, Letter no. 283 of 5 April 1769.

[16] In a different context the fluidity of political appropriations of the Spartacus image was shown by the success in America of the play *The Gladiator* by Robert Montgomery Bird. This was staged more that 1,000 times between 1831 and 1854 and lauded the democratic freedom of the American citizen.

[17] K. Marx, *Letter to Engels*, London February 27th 1861, translated and quoted in Shaw (2001), 14–15 on which this discussion is based.

[18] A. Koestler, *The Gladiators*, tr. Edith Simon (London, 1939; 2nd edition New York, 1956; 1962 – and with new postscript – New York, 1965).

direction from that in Germany. Karl Marx had compared Spartacus with the events of the Civil War in the United States and also with the achievements of Garibaldi, the decisive military figure in the movement for Italian freedom and unification in the nineteenth century. Following the example of the French revolutionaries, classicising imagery had been incorporated into the oratory, decrees, coinage and ceremonies developed by the Italian radicals and in 1874 Raffaello Giovagnoli published an historical novel *Spartaco*. Giovagnoli had fought with Garibaldi and his novel included substantial documentation from the ancient sources while adding a fictional encounter between Julius Caesar and Spartacus, to represent the opposition between tyranny and freedom. As well as supporting the nationalist agenda the rhetoric of the novel was also anti-clerical in tone.

Giovagnoli's approach resonated with the climate of Italian cinematic production in the early twentieth century.[19] Film production was seen as a means of enhancing Italian prestige and identity, as economically beneficial and as a way of inspiring the patriotism of mass audiences. The film *Quo Vadis?* (1913) was an enormous success and stimulated demand.[20] The film based on *Spartaco*, directed by Giovanni Enrico Vidali, also appeared in 1913, after Giovagnoli had been involved in the publication of a pamphlet in 1907 celebrating the centenary of Garibaldi's birth and associating him with the qualities of Spartacus. Vidali's new film altered the tragic ending of the novel to present Spartacus as triumphant and able to unite Italy. This aligned the film with the history of the movement for unification and thus obviated the risk that Spartacus' resistance to Crassus' cruelty might be thought to attack the current Italian regime. Another film on the subject, again called *Spartaco*, was released in 1952, directed by Riccardo Freda, following the serialization of Giovagnoli's novel in the weekly magazine of the Italian Communist Party.[21]

The cinematic history of refiguration of the Spartacus story illustrates very clearly the way in which successive appropriations held a balance

---

[19] For detailed discussion see Maria Wyke, *Projecting the Past: Ancient Rome, Cinema and History* (New York and London, 1997), esp. ch. 3 'Spartacus: testing the strength of the Body Politic', 34–72.

[20] For discussion of this film see M. Wyke, 'Screening Ancient Rome in the New Italy' in C. Edwards (ed.), *Roman Presences: Receptions of Rome in European Culture, 1789–1945* (Cambridge, 1999), 188–205.

[21] This may have been inspired by the posthumous publication of the prison notebooks of Antonio Gramsci in six volumes 1948–51. Mussolini had imprisoned Gramsci in the 1930s and his notebooks recorded his sense of the cultural and political value of Giovagnoli's novel if the style of presentation could be updated; discussed by Wyke (1997), 48–9.

between celebration and critique of contemporary political movements and regimes. This is particularly evident in the 1960 Kubrick/Douglas version. In her study of the making of the film Wyke points out that the technology (Super Technirama, Technicolour) not only permitted epic battle scenes and elaborate costumes but also employed a large number of actors.[22] *Spartacus* was proclaimed the most expensive film yet made in Hollywood under union conditions of employment, and union leaders co-operated in exhorting their members to see it. Within the film itself the scenes in the mines and gladiatorial school portray brutal working conditions which exploit human beings for the wealth and entertainment of the ruling class. The values implicit in the contrast are paralleled by the distinction between the two armies. The rebels are idealized, displaying the qualities of sharing and solidarity (when threatened with death they do not betray their leader, they all proclaim 'I'm Spartacus') while the Romans operate like robots, obedient to the hierarchy of wealthy political leaders. Speech rhythms and accent also carried implications for class and national identities and their associated values – for example, the American intonation of Douglas and Curtis contrasted with the 'theatrical English' speech by Olivier as the oppressor Crassus.

There was also some acknowledgement of the emphasis in Fast's novel on civil rights, especially in the fictional figure of Draba, the African gladiator who pays with his life for his refusal to kill Spartacus in the arena and thus inspires revolt. Kirk Douglas' autobiography (1988) extends this application by revealing how as the son of a Russian Jewish refugee he identified with oppressed slaves because of his race. This is perhaps reflected in the fact that in the film, although not in the novel, Spartacus is portrayed as the leader of a return of slaves back to their homelands rather than as destroyer of the power of the state.[23] However, the film was also made open to Christian and conservative interpretation. At the end the crucified Spartacus was shown with his newborn son and the child's mother, lit as for a biblical scene, while the subsequent voice-over says that the pagan tyranny of Rome was eventually replaced by a new and Christian society. In parallel, the heroism of Spartacus was also interpreted in Cold-War rhetoric as a stand against Soviet-style autocracy.[24]

[22] Wyke (1997), 65–72.

[23] Douglas presumably had a major influence on this adaptation since he was co-producer of *Spartacus* for his own company in conjunction with backing from the Hollywood studio Universal-International. The project was costed at 12 million dollars.

[24] *Variety*, 7th October 1960.

As a case study in reception approaches, the image of Spartacus demonstrates how figures and issues that were marginalized in their own time can later be given new kinds of prominence, both within antiquity and subsequently, in sympathy with cultural, political and (especially in the case of film) technological shifts. The case also shows that unquestioning association between, on the one hand, the values of the Roman Republic with asceticism and 'freedom' and, on the other hand, those of the Empire with luxury and oppression is deeply flawed (the Republican concept of *libertas* referred only to the status and independence of the senatorial class). Above all, the case shows that comparison of a range of receptions with the original sources is always fruitful in explaining the significance of shifts in reception.

The appropriation of Rome by Fascist and Nazi ideology

The case-study of Spartacus showed that political regimes and cultural movements of different kinds may compete to demonstrate 'ownership' of the same virtues and to deprecate the same vices. The attitude of Mussolini and Hitler to the Roman Empire shows that appropriation may also radically transpose what is understood by virtue and vice.

In 1922, as his Fascist militia prepared to march on Rome, Mussolini made a speech in which he claimed: 'Rome is our starting point – and our point of reference . . . We dream of a Roman Italy, that is to say wise and strong, disciplined and imperial . . . the fasces are Roman, Roman our organisation of combatants, Roman our pride and our courage. *Civis Romanus sum*'.[25] This belief had three main implications. The first was an emphasis on different aspects of Roman achievement at different stages of Mussolini's career. The second was the use of visual culture and theatre to communicate Roman models for the present. The third was the development of a fascist rhetoric of *romanità*. Historians have identified three main stages in the development of Mussolini's regime, and in connection with each there were adaptations in the exploitation of the association with ancient Rome.

From the establishment of Mussolini's power base in 1922 until the proclamation of the dictatorship in 1925, ancient Rome was

---

[25] Reported in the fascist newspaper *Il popolo d'Italia*, 21 April 1922; translated and quoted Maria Wyke, 'Sawdust Caesar: Mussolini, Julius Caesar and the drama of dictatorship', in M. Wyke and M. Biddiss (edd..), *The Uses and Abuses of Antiquity* (Bern, Berlin, Bruxelles, Frankfurt, New York, Wien, 1999), 167–86.

appropriated as a model for current political and military organization and as a symbol of Italian unity. Then the image of Rome took a new direction during the invasion of Abyssinia and the declaration of an Italian Empire in 1936. In the third phase in the late 1930s a climate of increasing racism was created and the Romans and the Latin language were used to define the supposed physical and spiritual and cultural superiority of the modern Italians. The whole process was underpinned by a programme of archaeological excavations, exhibitions and exploitation of revisionist classical scholarship, although as Wyke points out in her discussion of this phenomenon wider dissemination was through public visual and theatrical experience rather than through academic means.[26] As Eric Hobsbawm observed, the exercise of power became a public drama.[27] Visual imagery included use of the inscription SPQR, the *fasces*, eagles, Romulus and Remus she-wolves, battle standards, legionaries, the marching step, triumphal arches and columns; and after the war in Ethiopia the emphasis became increasingly militaristic with Roman domination of the Mediterranean, Aegean and North Africa used as justification for Mussolini's aims for imperial expansion, which were described as actions to recover land historically belonging to Italy.[28]

The policy was pursued through many exhibitions, the largest of which was the 1937 celebration of the two thousandth anniversary of the birth of Augustus, the *Mostra augustea della romanitá*. The effect of the exhibition was to present Mussolini's fascist empire as a modern equivalent to that of Augustus, who was depicted as empire-builder, peacemaker and warrior and paired with Mussolini in the statues at the entrance. The exhibition marked a shift away from Mussolini's earlier emphasis on Julius Caesar, to whom Mussolini had erected bronze statues in Rome and in Rimini (from where Caesar had launched his march on Rome after crossing the Rubicon).[29] An even larger exhibition, the Esposizione universale di Roma, was planned for 1942 to commemorate the twentieth year of the fascist regime and the fifth year

---

[26] Wyke (1999), 168.

[27] E. Hobsbawm, Forward to D. Ades, T. Benton, D. Elliott and I.B. Whyte (edd.), *Art and Power: Europe under the Dictators 1930–1945* (Hayward Gallery Exhibition Catalogue, Manchester, 1995), 11–15.

[28] For discussion of research into how fascism developed earlier aspects of the concept of *romanitá* see Marla Stone, 'A flexible Rome: Fascism and the cult of *romanitá*' in Catharine Edwards (ed.) (1999), 188–220.

[29] See further Ray Laurence, 'Tourism, town planning and *romanitá*: Rimini's Roman heritage', in Wyke and Biddiss (edd.) (1999), 187–205.

Fig. 4 Italian terracotta by Antonio Canova (1757–1822). Maria Luisa Hapsburg, wife of Napoleon Buonaparte, who was Canova's patron, depicted as Concordia. *Concordia* was one of the concepts used in the public art and literature of the Roman Empire to sanction imperial rule. Concordia's companion piece depicts *Pax*. Photo: National Gallery of Scotland, Edinburgh.

of empire. It was to include temporary exhibitions and permanent monuments such as the Palace of Italian Civilization, a square Colosseum with 216 arches. However, construction was suspended in 1941 because of World War II, leaving a marble skeleton which was to be subsequently transformed into offices.[30]

During the 1930s Italian fascism became more closely allied with Nazi Germany and radical adjustments to the concept of *romanità* introduced a strong racial component, especially after the war in Ethiopia. Africans and other political opponents were depicted as barbarian or sub-human. In 1938 anti-Semitic Racial Laws were passed and the propaganda attacked Jews as barbarians who presented a threat to the neo-Roman empire. This racialization of *romanità* was furthered by the film *Scipione l'Africano* (1937), directed by Carmine Gallforie. The film depicted the Carthaginians as uncivilized in behaviour and black and Semitic in appearance and represented the wars between Rome and Carthage as a conflict between authoritarian unity and anarchy. The film was awarded the top prize, the *Duce* cup, at the 1937 Venice Biennale Film festival but was widely held to be an artistic failure.

Initially, Mussolini's rhetoric of *romanità* seems to have found some favour in the United States. Hearst Movietone News in 1934 (November 21st) included footage entitled 'All Rome Hails City's Rebirth' with military music and a commentary on the ceremony at which 25,000 fascist athletes saluted 'their miracle man Mussolini. They celebrate the rejuvenation of ancient Rome, dug from its ruins, under the direction of Italy's modern Caesar'.[31]

However, the invasion of Ethiopia began to change opinion and allowed the publication of a scathing attack on Mussolini, who was mocked as a 'Sawdust Caesar' in a book by the journalist George Seldes.[32] A production of Shakespeare's *Julius Caesar* in 1937 (11th November, Mercury Theatre, New York), directed by Orson Welles drew on the association of Julius Caesar with tyranny and presented the play in modern dress with Joseph Holland as Caesar surrounded by bodyguards and Welles as Brutus played as a liberal politician in a suit. Press reviews commented on Holland's resemblance to Mussolini in

---

[30] See further T. Benton, 'Rome reclaims its Empire : Architecture' and 'Speaking without Adjectives : Architecture in the service of totalitarianism' in Ades *et al.* (edd.) (1995), 120–8.

[31] Hearst Movietone News Collection in the Film/TV Archive at UCLA, quoted and discussed by Wyke (1999), 175–6.

[32] G. Seldes, *Sawdust Caesar: the Untold History of Mussolini and Fascism* (New York and London, 1935).

gesture and appearance and at the start Caesar appeared in fascist uniform.[33] Eventually, the coup which deposed Mussolini was presented by Italians as the equivalent of the Ides of March. Hearst Movietone News took up Seldes' image of the 'Sawdust Caesar' in the changed circumstances of 1943 (27th July) in which Mussolini was portrayed as a clown. The final irony was delayed until 1945 when Mussolini was killed (28th April) and an undated cartoon was belatedly published which depicted him as Caesar with a clown's nose (designed by T.H. Heine for the Monaco magazine *Simplicissimus*).

By this time Mussolini's refiguration of *romanitá* had marginalized its Christian elements in order to exploit the iconography and architecture associated with Roman power. Reactions to the Mussolini/Caesar alignment included ridicule as well as focus on the counter-text provided by the historical figure of the tyrannicide Brutus. The selectivity practised by the Nazi régime in Germany took on some rather different aspects and emphasized racism even more strongly. However, Rome was not the only aspect of the ancient world that attracted Hitler. His sense of the importance of buildings as symbolic statements of power led him to admire the architecture of ancient Greece and he was said (by his architect and Arms Factory Minister Albert Speer) to have compared himself with Pericles, presumably drawing on the association between buildings, display of power and lasting reputation which was attributed to Pericles by Thucydides in the Funeral Speech[34] but neglecting Thucydides' stress on the Athenians' inconvenient insistence on Pericles' accountability to the Assembly.[35] However, the example of Sparta was more important to Hitler's regime than that of Athens because it offered, he thought, a paradigm of the rule by a minority of pure racial descent and high eugenic quality since its social customs and structure ensured the survival only of the fittest. In April 1945 Hitler *Jugend* formations including many fourteen-year-old boys called up for active service, and about to be sent on their bicycles to attack Soviet tanks, were lectured by the Nazi youth leader Arthur Axman on the heroism of Sparta.[36] In the same month Luftwaffe suicide missions were

[33] For full documentation and detailed discussion of the design and staging see Wyke (1999), 178–84.

[34] Thucydides, *History of the Peloponnesian War*, Book 2. 34–46, especially 41.

[35] Ibid., c.65. For discussion and full summary of recent research on Hitler's attitude to the ancient world, with bibliography, see Volker Losemann, 'The Nazi Concept of Rome' in Edwards (ed.) (1999), 221–35.

[36] An eye-witness account is quoted by Beevor (2002), 81. See also Theodore Ziolkowski, 'The Fragmented Text: the Classics and Post-war European Literature', *International Journal of the*

undertaken by the 'Leonidas squadron', an allusion to Spartan heroism at Thermopylae in 480 BCE against the invading Persians.

Nevertheless, there was a major shift away from the traditional German emphasis on Hellenism. Hitler thought that it was the history of Rome which offered the fullest models for the exercise of power and the development of policy and this interest has been documented from drafts of his early speeches.[37] He was impressed with Roman achievements in road building and military discipline and, presumably ignorant of the sources relating to the Romans' practices concerning cultural exchange and assimilation and religious syncretism, saw the empire as creating a monolithic civilization solely by the exercise of force. Hitler's volume *Table Talk*[38] suggests that he considered that it was Christianity which brought about the fall of the Roman Empire by ensuring the breakdown of status and citizenship divisions in a kind of pre-Bolshevik solidarity movement. He also associated the fall with the 'mobilization of the slave masses by the Jews', which he included in his conspiracy theory to account for the fall of Rome. He clung to history of the Roman 'example' right up to the end. His scorched-earth policy was named after Nero and in March 1945, in an initiative that would seem comic if it were not for the context, he ordered Goebbels, who was in charge of propaganda, to arrange for detailed discussions of the Punic Wars to appear once more in the newspapers. Already in 1944 in the face of military disaster the Second Punic War had been cited as an example of struggle against the 'Semitic trading people of Carthage' (*Völkischer Beobachter*, 20th September 1944). The phrase merged Jews and Carthaginians in the service of racist ideology and formed a parallel with the associations made in the Italian film *Scipione l'Africano* of 1937. Roman experiences in the Punic Wars were seen as a consolatory indication that defeat might eventually be followed by victory.

However, Nazification of ancient Rome encountered some difficulties not germane to the situation in fascist Italy, which for geographical and long-standing cultural reasons could look to Rome for foundation myths and continuity of tradition. Indeed, in 1934 Mussolini had expressed a sense of cultural superiority over Germany which, he said, represented a people which had lacked even literacy at a time when Rome had Caesar,

---

Classical Tradition, vol. 6 no. 4 (Spring 2000), 549–62, which discusses the pre-war Gymnasium curriculum in Prussia and the reception of the Thermopylae story in Herodotus by Schiller and Heinrich Böll.

[37] Discussed by Losemann (1999), 233

[38] A. Hitler, *Table Talk*, tr. N. Cameron and R.C.H Stevens (London, 1953).

Virgil and Augustus. This view found some currency in Germany in the 1930s in an influential article 'Die Antiker und wir' by a schoolteacher Walter Eberhardt. This was published in the *National Socialist Monthly* 6 in 1935 and criticized the Roman claim to world domination from a Germanic point of view – 'we think of the expeditions of Drusus and Tiberius and the punitive expedition of Germanicus and feel the wall which separates us from Roman cultural ideas'. Eberhardt was shortly afterwards appointed to a chair of Classics so presumably his opinions could be seen as a stimulus towards *aemulatio* of both ancient Germans and Romans and were not at that time contrary to those of the ruling clique. His article provoked others which competed in order to demonstrate the importance of classical languages, ancient history and archaeology for the Third Reich. A volume by the ancient historian Wilhelm Weber contributed to the debate by idealizing the *princeps* as a kind of Nietzschean superman. According to Weber the principate offered a system which could not only demonstrate the will to power but also tried to base itself on the purity of the past.[39]

It would be fair to point out that in terms of race theory, ancient historians outside Germany also showed interest in race mixture in the Roman Empire and some recent research has rehabilitated the reputations of ancient historians in Germany, especially those exiled to the United States and Britain. Some academics, particularly Hellenists who were less involved in the Nazi stress on *Römerwerte* (the value of Rome) made a principled decision to leave Germany.[40] The whole question of the co-operation or complicity of classicists and ancient historians in the appropriation of ancient history and iconography by totalitarian (or indeed other) political regimes is a salutary warning to any who are tempted to selectively emphasize crude relationships between ancient and modern in the hope of preserving interest in classical subjects, or who allow reception studies to become disengaged from critical enquiry into the relationship between the analogue ancient and modern texts or images.

From the cases discussed in this chapter it is clear that every example

---

[39] W. Weber, *Princeps: Studien zur Geschichte des Augustus* (Stuttgart, 1936).

[40] For an overview of research in this area, see Peter Lebrecht Schmidt, 'Latin Studies in Germany 1933–1945: Institutional Conditions, Political Pressures, Scholarly Consequences' in S.J. Harrison (ed.), *Texts, Ideas and the Classics* (Oxford, 2001), 285–300. Schmidt distinguishes various degrees of scholarly complicity with the Nazi regime. Also valuable is H. Lloyd-Jones, 'Interesting Times', *International Journal of the Classical Tradition*, vol. 4 no. 4 (Spring 1998), 580–613, with extensive footnotes and bibliographical references.

has its own reception history. Furthermore, appropriation of referents or the use of ancient models as *exempla* may take place in radical and revolutionary, as well as in conservative contexts. In addition, the ways in which Republican and Imperial Rome are characterized vary according to the context of appropriation and the battles for cultural 'ownership'. Even the same stereotype may be exploited in different ways in different contexts. *The Roman Actor* provokes spectators to question whether art actually makes any difference to moral insights or social action. The range of appropriations of Rome in architecture, film and educational and social policy in the twentieth century shows that the reception of classical material has been integrated as part of both propaganda and critique about public matters, including debates about national, social and political identities. Reception of classical material is a constituent part of this field of contest.

IV. STAGING RECEPTIONS

The focus of this chapter is on reception and staging, including opera, dance and physical theatre. There are two aspects of staging which raise crucial issues for reception studies. The first is that staging implies a live performance, a live audience. Each live performance is different and it is impossible to recapture it to allow the kind of analysis and debate about an established 'text' that is possible when discussing a poem or a painting. In fact, the task of the theatre historian in trying to reconstruct past performances has been compared with that of an art historian trying to study paintings solely on the basis of descriptions: 'One only needs to imagine what a history of painting would look like where the author had at his disposal neither originals nor copies of pictures but only any number of good descriptions! The historian of the theatre finds himself provisionally in just such a situation as soon as he leaves the realm of his own perception'.[1] In the 1920s when this distinction was drawn it was a radical one since it added to a historiographical approach, which was already shared with cognate areas of study, a new approach based on personal observation. This provided a counterweight to the transitory character of theatrical performance.

The effects of this shift of approach are seen in current reception studies in the methods used in the analysis of modern performances of ancient drama, whether in the original (with or without surtitles), in translation or in adaptation. The growth in the use of contemporary productions as research data for the study of reception is partly due to the widening of conceptions of what constitutes theatre 'history' and partly due to the sheer empirical pressure of the numbers of productions of ancient drama world-wide. These productions occur across the whole spectrum of theatre: student drama, touring companies, fringe and experimental productions, commercial theatre (including international tours by prestigious theatre companies and the attraction of élite companies to tourists).[2] This means that leading actors, writers,

---

[1] Julius Bat, *Das Theater der Gegenwart: Geschichte der dramatischer Bühne seit 1870* (Leipzig, 1928), 231 translated and discussed by Christopher B. Balme, 'Interpreting the Pictorial Record: Theatre Iconography and the Referential Dilemma' in *Theatre Research International* (Special Edition, Theatre and Iconography) vol. 22, no. 3 (1997), 180–201.

[2] In autumn 2002 the database of the Research Project on the *Reception of Greek Texts and Images in Late 20th Century Drama and Poetry in English* had recorded 606 examples covering the period

directors and designers become involved with ancient drama, and especially Greek drama, at various stages in their professional development. In many cases it has become an integral and distinctive part of their career. In recent years alone the directors Peter Stein, Peter Brook, Peter Hall and Deborah Warner have done major work on ancient theatre with actors such as Greg Hicks, Fiona Shaw and Diana Rigg (the last two have become 'stars' around whom productions with major female roles have centred) and designers Jocelyn Herbert, Dionysis Fotopoulos and Vicki Mortimer. These developments show that staging of ancient drama is not only a strand in the transmission of ancient culture but also a strand in current theatrical practice.

Sources for the analysis of live performance

In this respect, ancient drama is both a springboard for artistic and intellectual invention in staging and interpretation and a participant in the critique of modern theatrical forms and their social and political context. It is also in another sense itself a 'receiver' in that its theatrical vitality also makes it a conduit for engagement with the other theatrical activities and traditions which make up the history of performance of ancient drama. Combined with the transitory nature of all theatre this richness brings with it some problems for the research in reception of ancient drama. The range of primary sources which need to be used is large. In addition to the obvious sources of the ancient text and the performance text (whether an edited version in the original language or in a translation or adaptation) there have to be added the set design, lighting design, costume, movement and acting styles. Some aspects of the set and costumes may be archived by large companies but most of these aspects of performance are 'preserved' only through still photographs (sometimes posed for pre-performance publicity) and videos (often of poor quality and which direct the viewer's gaze from a crow's nest or an acute angle).[3] Posters and programmes often include useful visual and printed evidence about design, production values, the approach taken by the director and translator. A somewhat neglected area in reception research has been the extent of commercial sponsor-

from the 1970s to the beginning of the 21st century, with many more waiting to be documented. The data base can be searched at http://www2.open.ac.uk/ClassicalStudies/GreekPlays/.

[3] Unfortunately major studies of the constituent aspects of performance are rare. A notable exception is Jocelyn Herbert, *A Theatre Workbook*, (ed.) Cathy Courtney (London, 1993). This contains over 500 illustrations of Herbert's designs.

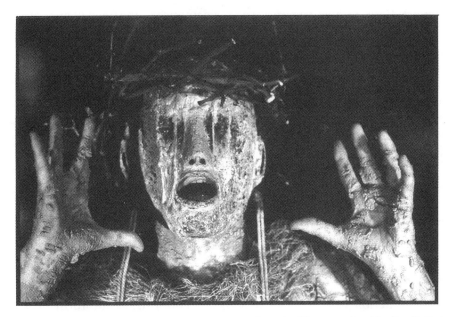

Fig. 5 Greg Hicks as Teiresias in Sophocles' *Oedipus the King*, translated by Ranjit Bolt and directed by Peter Hall, National Theatre, 1996. Hicks' role in Greek plays also include Orestes (*The Oresteia*, 1981), Agamemnon and Priam (*Tantalus* 2000/1) and Dionysus in *The Bacchai* (2002). Photo: Alan Titmuss.

ship, Arts Council and other grants and private subscriptions in enabling the production to be staged and perhaps toured.

Increasingly, these primary sources are augmented by use of the theatrical review and the interview. The theatrical review is a difficult type of source to use critically. This is partly because it is produced as part of the policy of the publishing newspaper or periodical and therefore reflects those priorities and assumptions about (for example) the extent of the knowledge or prejudices about the ancient world and about theatre which its target readership may have.[4] In addition, the theatrical review is a source of evidence about how the production was staged and the reactions of the audience. This performance 'narrative' is

---

[4] For a study of the social and cultural bias of the theatrical review as a source for theatre history, see L. Hardwick, 'The Theatrical Review as a Primary Source for the Modern Reception of Greek Drama: a Preliminary Evaluation' at http://www2.open.ac.uk/ClassicalStudies/Greek Plays/Webpages/Projectsite/ Reviews.html. A few major companies have co-operated in accounts of their work, for example Jonathan Croall, *Peter Hall's Bacchai: the National Theatre at Work* (London, 2002).

subject both to the vagaries and selectivity of the visual and aural memory of the reviewer and to his or her subjective judgements (which often colour an apparently factual description).

The theatrical interview is also becoming a significant oral and documentary source, particularly in recording the intentions and approach of the translator, director and actors. However, like the review it is by no means a neutral document. The focus and structure varies according to the type of publication (e.g. weekend broadsheet supplement, arts magazine, radio or TV news or arts programme, academic study or archive). Also important is the point in time at which the interview is conducted – during the rehearsal process, pre or post-performance, immediately after the run or later, when recollections may be coloured by the theatre practitioner's new work.[5]

Text and performance

In conjunction with the fact that the reception takes the form of live performance, the second aspect of staging which is crucial for reception studies is the relationship between text and performance. The text/ performance relationship has become the dominant factor in the approach to drama in its ancient context.[6] These investigations began by analysis of evidence within the texts of the plays, for instance on exits and entrances, movements and costume. Scholars then integrated this analysis with the extant visual evidence from ancient theatre sites, painted pottery, wall paintings and mosaics. Action research has also been developed to reconstruct and explore the implications of the use of masks, music and the choreography of the chorus in creating the ancient

[5] A critical study of the role of the theatre practitioner interview in reception research is being conducted by Alison Burke and will be published in 2003 at http://www2.open.ac.uk/ ClassicalStudies/GreekPlays/Webpages/essays/essaypage.htm.

[6] For Greek drama, the work of Oliver Taplin is central, especially *The Stagecraft of Aeschylus* (Oxford, 1977); *Greek Tragedy in Action* (London, 1978); *Comic Angels and Other Approaches to Greek Drama through Vase-Paintings* (Oxford, 1993), together with David Wiles, *Tragedy in Athens: Performance Space and Theatrical Meaning* (Cambridge, 1997), and *Greek Theatre Performance: an Introduction* (Cambridge, 2000). The study of the material environment is summarized in J.R. Green, 'Forty Years of Theatre Research and its Future Directions' in L. Hardwick, P.E. Easterling, S. Ireland, N. Lowe and F. Macintosh (edd.), *Theatre: Ancient and Modern* (Milton Keynes, 2000), 1–20. This has an extensive bibliography and is also available electronically at http://www.open.a-c.uk/Arts/CC99/ green.html. For study of the Roman theatre, the best starting point is R.C. Beacham, *The Roman theatre and its audience* (London, 1995), together with Peter G. McC. Brown, 'Actors and actor-managers at Rome in the time of Plautus and Terence' in P. Easterling and E. Hall (edd.), *Greek and Roman Actors: Aspects of an Ancient Profession* (Cambridge, 2002), 225–237.

Fig. 6 Maria Fierheller as Hecuba, holding Astyanax (in a bag of dust) in *Trojan Women*, adapted and directed by David Stuttard, Actors of Dionysus, 2002. Photo: Dave Ashton.

theatrical experience.[7] This aspect of ancient theatre research also has a vital role in reception studies since it both provides a framework for comparison between ancient and subsequent performances and is also stimulated by reception research which may generate new questions to be asked about ancient staging. In research into both ancient and modern staging, the question of the audiences and their reactions presents particular difficulties. In neither case is it possible to reconstruct other than indirectly the variety of perspectives that members of the audiences brought to, or took away from, the performance – the ancient audiences and those of the intervening centuries are no longer there to be asked and modern audience research has not been systematically undertaken. In antiquity some judgements may be made about audience numbers and their likely social and cultural horizons and in

---

[7] See Fiona Macintosh's discussion of the inaudibility of the masked actors in the 1981 production of Tony Harrison's translation of *The Oresteia*, directed by Peter Hall, in F. Macintosh, 'Tragedy in Performance: Nineteenth- and Twentieth-century Productions' in P.E. Easterling (ed.), *The Cambridge Companion to Greek Tragedy* (Cambridge, 1997), 24–323 and D. Wiles, 'The Use of Masks in Modern Performances of Greek Drama' in E. Hall, F. Macintosh and A. Wrigley (edd.), *Dionysus since '69* (Oxford, 2003).

post-antiquity there are some personal anecdotes.[8] It is generally agreed
by researchers that modern audiences are more culturally diverse than
those in antiquity. They are less likely to be aware of the ancient myths
and therefore less likely to be sensitive to the ways in which either these
myths or the theatrical conventions of ancient performance are being
adapted for the stage. Their 'horizons of expectation' may differ quite
substantially from each other as well as from audiences in antiquity. The
consequences for performance of Greek comedy are particularly acute in
that the specific references to contemporary political figures in Old
Comedy are difficult to communicate on the modern stage. In New
Comedy and Roman comedy the stock figures and situations are more
easily transferable across time and place. Where the nuances of the
ancient text are not well known, modern performance has both to
orientate the audience and to provide other theatrical means of explaining the significance of what is happening. This puts a particular
premium on the relationship between verbal and non-verbal languages
of performance.[9]

Verbal and non-verbal languages of performance

The study of the reception of ancient drama has therefore drawn on
broader aspects of analysis of the semiotics (or sign-systems) of theatre.
Theatrical semiotics generally distinguishes between:

(i)   Language-based signs, that is, words, the sequences and
      patterns in which they are used and the ideas which they
      express.

(ii) Para-linguistic signs which are connected both to linguistic
      signs and to the non-verbal signs which directly communicate
      meaning. Examples would be vocal sounds used to move the
      audience to sadness, anger or excitement or to communicate
      the feelings or identity of the speaker – emphasis and tone and
      regional accent would be good examples. These para-linguistic
      elements are important in staging ancient drama for their

---

[8] For ancient evidence, see E. Csapo and W.J. Slater, *The Context of Ancient Drama* (Michigan,
1995).

[9] Recent scholarship has broadened this study to explore the relationship with other aspects of
performance culture in religion, politics and social practices; see S. Goldhill and R. Osborne (edd.),
Performance Culture and Athenian Democracy (Cambridge, 1999), and D. Wiles, 'Theatre in Roman
and Christian Europe' in J.R. Brown (ed.), *The Oxford Illustrated History of Theatre* (Oxford, 1995),
49–92.

contribution in 'translating the untranslatable' such as sounds of lament or juxtaposition of regional or ethnic differences. These aspects may generate a code or system within the play or use codes outside the play, thus narrowing the gap between the alien aspects of ancient drama and the experiences of the (assumed) audience.

(iii)   Kinesic signs – these include facial and body movements and include sub-groups such as mimic signs, gestures and proxemic signs (that is those that interact with the space around them, showing distance or proximity for example, or which take the shape of movement). There is considerable debate about the extent to which universal validity can be attributed to the connection between facial expression and emotion. This problem has special implications for modern performances of Greek drama if masks are not used. Equally, there is debate about the universality of gesture signs, again important for ancient drama where expressions of · supplication or lament might be involved.[10]

(iv)   Actors' appearance – mask, hairstyle, costume.

(v)   Spatial signs – theatrical space and situation and stage space which includes set, lighting and properties.

(vi)   Non-verbal acoustic signs – including non-verbal sounds and music.

All of these types of sign are involved in transforming the written text into the theatrical text of the performance. The conventional term 'translation on to the stage' includes all these elements and has to be distinguished both from 'translation for the stage' (which refers to the creation of a written text that can be performed) and from the growing broader connotations of the word 'translation' which is sometimes used to indicate movement from one cultural location to another.

Historical and process-based approaches

The discussion so far has drawn on two main models for studying reception on the stage. The first is the performance history which studies the staging of a particular play through time (*diachronic*). This

---

[10] For a detailed discussion of theatrical semiotics and associated research on universality and cultural specificity, see Erika Fischer-Lichte, *The Semiotics of Theatre*, tr. Jeremy Gaines and Doris L. Jones (Bloomington and Indianapolis, 1992) (originally published in three volumes in 1983 as *Semiotik des Theaters* (Tübingen)).

approach has strengths in enabling comparisons in staging of plays to be
made that draw on the similarities and differences in how and why
different periods select ancient plays for staging and interpret their
meaning.[11] Depending on the sources available it is not always possible
to compare details of performances and the emphasis may sometimes be
on the broader cultural and economic conditions governing the performance. The other main model used for studying stage reception
concentrates on the processes of creating a particular production at a
particular time (*synchronic*). Different kinds of sources are needed in
order to study the performance itself and to situate it in the broader
contexts of the theatrical careers of the practitioners, the conditions
which generate the production, and the reactions of audiences and
critics. In the case of very recent performances, sufficient time may not
have elapsed to make judgements about the significance of the production in the performance history of the play.

The coherent study of reception on the stage of course requires both
diachronic and synchronic models to be considered and they are
increasingly being used in conjunction with one another. A good
example of this tendency is the volume published by the Oxford Archive
of Performance of Greek and Roman Drama, *Medea in Performance
1500–2000*.[12] This includes a table of performances as well as the
individual essays which trace the history of production of the play
through the Renaissance, the eighteenth century and the Victorian stage
as well as in the twentieth century in a variety of political situations,
several cultural traditions and other genres such as opera and film.
Another example of the convergence between diachronic and synchronic studies is the volume *Tragic Consequences* in preparation by the Open
University project on *The Reception of the Texts and Images of Ancient
Greece in Modern Drama and Poetry*. This studies the ways in which
selected plays were refigured in antiquity and in mediating contexts such
as French classical theatre and analyses the impact of modern theatre
companies, directors and designers on cultural aspects of reception.

The historical and process-based approaches also converge in their
use of categories and frameworks for describing and evaluating staging
in comparison with other performances within antiquity and subsequently. These can be summarized as follows:

---

[11] See the analysis of Greek plays on the twentieth-century American stage in relation to periods
of war and peace in Karelisa V. Hartigan, *Greek Tragedy on the American Stage* (Westport CT,
1995).

[12] E. Hall, F. Macintosh and O. Taplin (edd.), *Medea in Performance 1500–2000* (Oxford, 2000).

(i) Language – including text and translation and also the variety and registers with the play.
(ii) Use of ancient conventions – mask, chorus, formal elements such as *agon*, *rhêsis*, *stichomythia*, messenger-narrative, panto-mime.
(iii) Time, place, culture – setting is crucial in decisions about whether the play is to be moved into the world of the audience or the audience moved into the world of the play or whether the play aims to open up a situation related to both the world of the original and that of the audience.[13]
(iv) Context of production – on the spectrum between public festival and house-theatre, including court performance, music hall.
(v) Context of performance – theatre space and its environment.
(vi) Critical reception – from victory in a publicly judged com-petition to premature cancellation of the run because of unfavourable reaction from audiences and critics.

Underlying these lines of enquiry there are also broader questions about the patterns of revival – including the selection of the play at a particular time and its prominence in particular kind of social or cultural situation.

Original language receptions

The history of ancient plays performed in the original language provides some important insights into reception histories. This is particularly the case in respect of Greek plays in which, from the late nineteenth century there has been significant interaction between amateur and professional contexts. The University of Edinburgh started a trend with the pro-duction of Greek plays in translation from 1873. In 1880 Aeschylus' *Agamemnon* was staged in Greek at Oxford and involved collaboration between budding professional theatre practitioners such as Frank Benson, the Master of Balliol Benjamin Jowett, and W. B. Richmond who painted the scenery. Benson went on to perform in the inaugural Greek play at Bradfield College in 1891 (Euripides' *Alcestis*). The

---

[13] Furthermore, re-location of key debates to a supposedly neutral setting has been proven to be a good way of defeating censorship. See Anthony Meech, 'The Irrepressible in Pursuit of the Impossible, Translating the Theatre of the GDR' in Carole-Anne Upton (ed.), *Moving Target: Theatre Translation and Cultural Relocation* (Manchester, 2000), 127–37 and L. Hardwick, *Translating Words, Translating Cultures* (London, 2000), ch. 4 'Translation as Critique and Intervention'.

Cambridge Greek play was inaugurated in 1882 (with a production of Sophocles' *Ajax*) and the tradition still flourishes.

The initial approach in Cambridge was to base the productions closely on assumptions then current in classical archaeology concerning the construction of the sets. In addition the music seems to have been a great attraction, and special trains were laid on from London.[14] The initiative found parallels in the United States with *Oedipus the King* staged in Greek (Harvard 1881 and Notre Dame 1888) and in Australia (University of Sydney, *Agamemnon*, 1886).[15] Although it was difficult to sustain the initial impetus (the transfer of the Oxford *Agamemnon* to London in 1880 was seen by Henry Irving and Ellen Terry as well as George Eliot), the Oxford, Cambridge and Bradfield projects continued to have an impact on the reception of Greek drama on the stage in Britain. In the later part of the twentieth century Bradfield attracted the attention of the director Peter Hall and the traditions at Oxford and Cambridge probably contributed to the twentieth-century trend of inviting distinguished classicists to advise on the staging of classical drama on the commercial stage. The 'archaeological' focus of the Cambridge Greek play did not, however, persist. The more recent productions have included imaginative sets and have emphasized resonances that cross time and place. The production of Sophocles' *Electra* in 2001, directed by the classicist and theatre practitioner Jane Montgomery, did not have a Greek setting and made use of modern technology such as video screens which were used to illustrate the childhood histories of Electra and Orestes. It also used English surtitles, as did the Oxford University Dramatic Society *Medea* in the same year. This production, directed by Nat Coleman, who was then an undergraduate in Classics, did retain the Greek setting, emphasizing this by costume and body make-up designs derived from Greek vase paintings. These examples of recent original language productions, which have attracted large and varied audiences, differ in their approaches to the relationship between ancient text and modern performance. They share, however, an appreciation that audiences for performances in the original language are not confined to those who either have a good knowledge of

---

[14] For the development of the history of the Cambridge Greek play, see P.E. Easterling 'Greek Plays at Cambridge' in *Le Théâtre Antique de Nos Jours : Symposium International à Delphes 18–21 Août 1981* (Athens), 89–94 and 'The early years of the Cambridge Greek play' in C.A. Stray (ed.), *Classics in Nineteenth and Twentieth Century Cambridge: Curriculum, Culture and Community*, PCPS Supplement 24 (Cambridge, 1999), 27–47.

[15] For further discussion, see Macintosh in Easterling (ed.) (1997).

the language or are at least well informed about the plays and their theatrical contexts.

Translated receptions

This sense of the need to seek out wider audiences has been even more developed in productions which are staged in translation. The stress on performance as well as text and the effect on the way in which productions are discussed and evaluated has become known as the 'performative turn'. In terms of the translation approaches used I would take this further and describe it as the 'performative slide', in which even relatively close translations are shaped by the demands of performance.[16] Translations prepared specifically for the stage naturally have to have particular regard for speakability and performability. The actors must not only feel able to speak the lines with confidence but must also be able to move to them (in terms of rhythm and pacing). Modern productions in English have eschewed 'distancing' or 'foreignizing' approaches to translation and have aimed for the play to read and sound as if it were originally written in English. Just as important is the changed composition of audiences. Many spectators have only the most general idea of the plot and conventions of the plays and are certainly in no position to be able draw conclusions about the impact of cuts, revisions or adaptations made from the original. In many cases, these factors combine to bring about an increased degree of interpretation and explanation within the production. This may take both verbal and non-verbal forms in order to create or restore some 'referential validity' to the classical framework as a 'language' for receiving and interpreting the play. Examples of the effect of this priority occur not only in 'free' translations but also in those which follow the ancient text quite closely. In his translation of *Agamemnon* (1999 version) David Stuttard, a trained classicist who worked closely from Fraenkel's edition, developed the images of blossoming and decay beyond the role given them by Aeschylus. The Herald describes the Aegean sea on the morning after the storm destroys the fleet:

And when the sun broke through at dawn, the whole Aegean sea was blossoming with shipwrecks and the corpses of the dead.[17]

---

[16] See L. Hardwick, '*Electra* and the Theatre of Affliction: towards a textual turn?', *Didaskalia*, special edition on Sophocles' *Electra*, vol. 5 no. 3 (2002), published electronically at www.didaskalia.net.

[17] Aeschylus, *Agamemnon*, lines 658–9; D. Stuttard, *Agamemnon* (York, 1999), 12.

Later, Agamemnon describes Cassandra as 'my flower, my blossom' and Stuttard thought that the audience would be prepared by the earlier image to pick up the sinister undertones here.[18] In his version Stuttard also makes Clytemnestra use the image in her 'welcome' to Agamemnon – 'and now you are here like warmth in winter, thawing out our house to make it blossom'.[19] R.L. Lattimore[20] translates this as 'you bring with you the symbol of our winter's warmth', while Lloyd-Jones has 'you signal warmth in the winter by your coming'.[21] Finally Clytemnestra in her triumphant speech after the murders comments on her struggle for vengeance 'now in time and with eternal justice it has flowered to its fulfilment'.[22] This variation on the theme follows from Stuttard's view that Aeschylus' major challenge to the translator is the need to preserve and communicate the tension between symbol and reality in the imagery. The multiplication of the image is intended to ensure that the audience, unfamiliar with Aeschylus' imagery, does not miss the structural force of the metaphor.[23]

Relationships with the language of reception

Other approaches to translating for the stage have shown various kinds of assimilation into the new language. Two which are particularly important are those in which the receiving language and cultural framework dominates the interpretation and those in which the receiving language is infused with an additional conceptual and emotional range. Examples of the first kind of assimilation are often signalled by anachronisms. A production of *Trojan Women* in the spring of 2002 demonstrates this. The chorus refers to the sufferings of 'the Lebanon and Palestine, Uzbekistan, Afghanistan, Croatia, Kosovo – an old world butchered in a blaze of ashes'.[24] Then Hekabe picks up the refrain and the chorus refers to 'The towers exploding in a holocaust of flame' (23). In contrast, in her translation of Euripides' lines 1320–1, Shirley Barlow has 'The dust like smoke winging to the sky shall prevent me from seeing

---

[18] Source: interview with David Stuttard, March 2001.
[19] Aeschylus, *Agamemnon*, lines 968–9.
[20] R.L. Lattimore *The Oresteia* (Chicago, 1954).
[21] H. Lloyd-Jones, *Aeschylus: Oresteia* (London, 1982).
[22] Aeschylus, *Agamemnon*, lines 1377–8; Stuttard (1999), 26.
[23] For further discussion of translations of *Agamemnon* see L. Hardwick, 'Staging *Agamemnon*: the languages of translation' in F. Macintosh (ed.), *Agamemnon Staged: Proceedings of the Agamemnon Conference 2001* (Oxford, 2003/4).
[24] D. Stuttard, Acting Script for *Trojan Women* (York, 2002), 16.

my home' and 'the sound of the towers falling'.[25] The 2002 acting script's allusions to recent events, including the terrorist attack on the twin towers of the World Trade Centre in New York on 11th September 2001, received some criticism for restricting audience autonomy in their reception of the play. On reflection the translator expressed some doubts about the use of specific names but considered that the imagery of the collapse of the towers was an equivalent to that in Euripides.[26]

The impact of the classical referential framework and its linguistic registers on the receiving language is a feature of recent translations into Scots. In 1990 the first act of *Klytemnestra's Bairns*, a translation by Bill Dunlop of Aeschylus' *Agamemnon*, was staged at the Edinburgh Festival Fringe. The full text of the complete *Oresteia* was later performed on Calton Hill.[27] Dunlop added a prologue by Apollo to explain to the audience the situation of the inherited curse of the House of Atreus and to accustom them to the idiom he was using. In his 'afterword' Dunlop situated his version in a tradition ranging from John Stuart Blackie and Gilbert Murray to Robert Lowell and Tony Harrison, adding 'This adaptation imagines a possible response to a request from a financially constrained Athens for an accessible cost-effective reworking of the text, making use of local varieties of language'. This is a reference to the regional varieties of lowland Scots. Dunlop also published a study of the process of creating his translation, starting from the premise that 'Any translation or adaptation into Scots is, perforce, a political act which asserts the validity of [the] language'.[28] Dunlop deliberately chose the area of ancient tragedy in order to produce a translation which would mediate between the literary and the everyday. He particularly wished to develop the range of modern Scots to 'Allow it to discuss intellectual concepts in a currently acceptable form', building on the strength of Scots which he saw as 'its immediacy, its ability to hit emotional targets with remarkable precision and concision, and, despite its limitations in carrying complex intellectual cargoes, its flexibility of response to altered circumstances'.

In common with the creators of many modern versions Dunlop worked from other translations, being most influenced by Lowell and Vellacott.[29]

---

[25] S. Barlow (ed., tr. and commentary), *Euripides, Trojan Women* (Warminster, 1986).

[26] Source: interview with David Stuttard, August 2002.

[27] Published text: Bill Dunlop, *Klytemnestra's Bairns* (Edinburgh, 1993).

[28] Bill Dunlop, 'Klytemnestra's Bairns : Adapting Aeschylus into Scots', *International Journal of Scottish Theatre*, vol. 1 no. 1 (2000) (http://arts.qmuc.ac.uk/ijost/Volume1_no1/B_Dunlop.htm).

[29] Tr. Robert Lowell, *The Oresteia of Aeschylus* (New York, 1978) and tr. Philip Vellacott, *The Oresteian Trilogy* (Harmondsworth, 1959).

Dunlop's approach indicates the broader cultural significance of the revival of the Scots which was part of the literary revival of the earlier twentieth century as well as one manifestation of the climate of cultural nationalism surrounding devolution at the end of the century. It was felt that after the Treaty of Union in 1707 the varieties of the Scots language, celebrated by Gavin Douglas' translation of the *Aeneid* in 1513, had been devalued by the stress on English literary forms and at the end of the twentieth century there was a renewed interest in translating classical texts (both ancient and French) into Scots.[30] This development is being researched by Ian Brown, John Ramage and Ceri Sherlock in a project which compares the Scots and Welsh languages as vehicles for the translation of Greek myth into another culture in a way which is analogous to the translation of a text from one language into another. The project also analyses ways in which the Scots and Welsh languages are capable of dealing with the material of ancient tragedy, with special emphasis on *Antigone*.[31]

Reception of Comedy

One of the points made by Dunlop in his discussion of the theatrical strengths of the Scots language is its flexibility as a medium for irony, sarcasm and forms of humour that rely on juxtaposition of words and a sense of the ridiculous; and Scots has been used by a number of translators of comedy.[32]

Translation of comedy raises further questions about the relationship between language and performance and about the communication of equivalences. The problems about the differences in the cultural frame of reference between ancient and modern audiences are particularly acute in comedy because humour uses contemporary references as well as exploitation of the human situation for its effect. One approach to

---

[30] For further discussion see L. Hardwick, 'Classical Theatre in Modern Scotland – a Democratic Stage?' in L. Hardwick and C. Gillespie (edd.), *Crossing Boundaries through Greek Tragedy*, Selected Proceedings of the Open Colloquium (Milton Keynes, 2003).

[31] I. Brown and C. Sherlock, '*Antigone*, a Scots/Welsh Experience of Mythical and Theatrical Translation' in L. Bowker, M. Cronin, D. Kenny and J. Pearson (edd.), *Unity in Diversity? Current Trends in Translation Studies* (Manchester, 1998), 25–37 and I. Brown, J. Ramage and C. Sherlock, 'Scots and Welsh: Theatrical Translation and Theatrical Languages,' *International Journal of Scottish Theatre* vol. 1 no. 2 (2000), http://arts.qmuc.ac.uk/ijost/Volume1_no2/I_Brown.htm. On translation of Greek plays into Welsh see further L. Llewellyn-Jones, 'Trasidei Gymraeg: Is there a Classical Tradition in Welsh Language Drama?' in L. Hardwick and C. Gillespie (edd.) (2003).

[32] Notably Alan Sommerstein in his translation of Aristophanes, *Lysistrata* (London, 1973), in which the Spartans speak in Scots dialect.

such issues for the translator of Aristophanes has been summarized by Peter Meineck, a classicist and theatre practitioner, who translates specifically for performance – 'that sound scholarship is essential to any translation of an ancient play goes without saying, but what about the lessons learned from performance? A play is only created for performance and its existence as a written text is subordinate to its primary form and function as a live, shared experience between actors and audience. But can a contemporary, English-language production of an Aristophanes play, any more than a script that gives directions for one, still be called an experience of Aristophanes?'.[33]

Meineck's answer to this dilemma is that in spite of differences between contemporary and ancient theatre, both draw on experiences that still have dramatic force – father-and-son conflict, stupidities of the legal system, corruption of politicians, satire of new ideas, human problems and aspirations. However, he chose not to update the contemporary references in Aristophanes' plays on the grounds that 'A joke about a politician's errant behaviour in the news today will seem as out of date to an audience or reader in five years as will a reference to Cleon or Alcibiades'. His view was that a skilled actor and director can make references to ancient historical (or mythical) figures understood by the audience by facial expression, movement and body language. (This is not the same as *explaining* such references, which Meineck does in his printed text by a combination of footnotes and endnotes, an indication, perhaps, that performance is not quite all.)

A further challenge to the translators and performers of ancient comedy is the mobility of language (words, tone, register) within the texts. This element was discussed by Michael Silk in his major study of Aristophanes.[34] While acknowledging the importance of mobility of language in the Roman satirists (especially Petronius) Silk regards Aristophanes as the prime exponent. He contrasts this with classical tragedy and Menandrian comedy which are characterized by decorum, homogeneity and coherence from which it is difficult to deviate. Aristophanic comedy has, Silk concludes, its own coherence which incorporates diversity and freedom from the necessity to conform.[35] This mobility and diversity of language was, in the ancient world,

---

[33] P. Meineck, Translator's Preface, *Aristophanes* (*Clouds, Wasps, Birds*) (Indianapolis and Cambridge, 1998), xxxvii–viii.

[34] M. Silk, *Aristophanes and the Definition of Comedy* (Oxford, 2000), especially ch. 3 'Language and style'.

[35] Silk (2000), 158–9.

subversive and not the norm which might be expected by an English-speaking audience influenced by Shakespeare and subsequent dramatic traditions. Finding equivalences for the mobility of the Greek language is a fence too far for most translators and directors and is particularly difficult to achieve when the translation has adopted an approach based on acculturation, or bringing the text to the audience. One recent attempt is of particular interest in that it attempted to transpose mobility of language into mobility of movement.

Physicality as reception – movement, dance and the body

The production was that of Aristophanes' *Birds* in London in 2002 in a verse adaptation by Sean O'Brien.[36] The production which was directed by Kathryn Hunter, a leading exponent of physical theatre, was a collaboration between the Royal National Theatre and Mamaloucos Circus as part of the RNT's 'Transformation' season. The production, which was initially intended to be followed by a national tour in 'Big Top' venues, used the episodic structure of the play as a basis for exploring in movement the diverse linguistic registers of the successive visitors to Cloudcuckooland. The 'rapping' Poet, for example, gave a virtuoso display of break-dancing ('for those who think tradition's crap') while the chorus of birds themselves were played by trapeze artists and this allowed some virtuoso performances. However, the production had a mixed reception from critics.[37] One critic drew an analogy between O'Brien's verse – 'muscularity, flipping from coarse colloquialism and nonchalant rhyming couplets to an exalted lyricism' – and the evocation of the Birds – 'rippling torsos stand in for ornate plumage. Simple gestures – splayed hands, inclined heads and jerky limbs – conjure earthbound movements, while sundry feats of daring replicate the miracle of light' – but concluded 'there's only so much swinging on harnesses the eye can take'.[38] Other critics were more damning, referring to uneasy relationships between 'aerial athleticism and Aristophanic satire'[39] and the shift of satirical object from the Utopian aspirations in Aristophanes to the militaristic tyranny of Peisthetaerus (Pez in this version). Perhaps the problem

[36] Published text, S. O'Brien, *Aristophanes: Birds* (London, 2002).
[37] Partly because at three hours' duration the performance tested to the limit the audience's endurance of the cramped temporary seating at the Lyttleton Theatre.
[38] Dominic Cavendish, *The Daily Telegraph*, July 29th, 2002.
[39] Michael Billington, *The Guardian*, July 29th, 2002.

with the circus-based approach was that movement was used partly as spectacle partly as intermission. This both held up the narrative energy of the play and prevented integration with its nuances of meaning, language and humour (several critics described it as 'remarkably humourless').

In contrast, when used representationally, the body has been a key aspect of performance in several recent productions. These have restored to Greek drama the physicality which was an important aspect of ancient productions (especially since the use of masks required communication through gesture and body movement rather than facial expression and because the dancing space for the Chorus allowed and required careful choreography). An important example is the Jazzart Dance Theatre dancers who took the role of the Chorus in the production of *Medea* directed by Mark Fleishman and Jennie Reznek in South Africa in three seasons in Cape Town, Grahamstown and Johannesburg between 1994 and 1996. Jazzart Dance Theatre was the first South African multi-racial modern dance company. In this performance they drew on traditional forms of expression and also used creative improvisation as part of the rehearsal process.[40]

The principle of the Jazzart Company is that the actor's body is not just a vehicle for conveying meaning but can actually communicate nuances of the processes of struggle – through movement, caressing, revealing and even contortion and 'fracture'. In this production of *Medea* dance was a way of incorporating oral tradition and consciousness into the play and also of transcending language barriers. In a country where eleven languages have official status, verbal and somatic languages joined together to tell the story. In the Corinthian sequences the chorus impersonated Greeks, using contemporary jazz dance familiar in the West. In the Colchis scenes, they were transformed into ethnic Colchians, wearing tribal dress with African dance movements. Margaret Mezzabotta, the pioneer of performance analysis of Greek drama productions in South Africa, pointed out how this type of cultural interaction in performance provided a learning experience for the audience: 'Each of the linguistic visual and musical codes through which the performance communicated was interpreted with varying

---

[40] The use of movement at the rehearsal stage was also a feature of the RNT production of Euripides' *The Bacchai*, directed by Peter Hall in summer 2002, when both Greg Hicks as Dionysus and the members of the Chorus drew on Japanese *Butoh* techniques. However, this aspect was by no means fully integrated into the subsequent performances. See further Amanda Wrigley, 'Review of Royal National Theatre's *Bacchai*', *JACT Review*, second series, no. 32 (2002), 12–14.

degrees of ease by the individual members of the audience, depending on their cultural backgrounds' and suggested that this provided a metaphor for the difficulty of mutual understanding in post-apartheid South Africa, a difficulty which had gradually to be overcome through shared experiences.[41]

The Jazzart role in the South African *Medea* is one example of the way in which a combination of more that one art form can highlight a crucial and sometimes revolutionary change of direction in interpretation and artistic power in relation to a canonical or iconic work. Another example generated by ancient drama was the three-act ballet *Clytemnestra* created by the dance-choreographer Martha Graham and first performed in 1958. This included a few spoken fragments at key junctures (for instance when the sacrifice of Iphigenia is danced). Graham's version probed the psychology of Clytemnestra's story and heightened the emotional impact by the use of costume design drawn from black-figure vase paintings and the use of Eastern Mediterranean music to create an atmosphere of violence. It was suggested by one critic that Graham's Clytemnestra 'stands in the history of drama where Joyce's *Ulysses* stands in the history of the novel : it is as bold an experiment, as radical a departure'.[42]

Operatic receptions

The creators of opera in the Renaissance aimed to revive from antiquity the fusion of music and drama in one art form.[43] On the modern stage the treatment of classical plays in opera has been significant in bringing together art forms to express radical change. The impact of the first performance of Strauss's opera *Elektra* in London in 1910 has been explored by Simon Goldhill in a recent study.[44] Goldhill analysed how Hugo von Hofmannsthal's libretto, taken from his own play which had scandalized and enthralled Germany a few years previously, worked with Strauss's modernist music and, in offering a version of the Electra

[41] M. Mezzabotta, 'Ancient Drama in the New South Africa' in L. Hardwick *et al.* (edd.), *Theatre Ancient and Modern* (Milton Keynes, 2000), 246–68, 253.

[42] LeRoy Leatherman, *Martha Graham: Portrait of the Lady as an Artist*, quoted and discussed in J. Chioles, '*The Oresteia* and the *avant-garde* : three decades of discourse', *Performing Arts Journal*, no. 45 (1993), 1–28.

[43] For discussion see P. Burian, 'Tragedy adapted for stages and screens: the Renaissance to the present' in Easterling (ed.), 1997, 228–83, esp. 261–71.

[44] S. Goldhill, 'Blood from the shadows: Strauss' disgusting, degenerate *Elektra*', in *Who Needs Greek? Contests in the Cultural History of Hellenism* (Cambridge, 2002), 108–77.

story 'full of blood and violence and sexual perversion', challenged the investments of national cultures in ideals derived from the Greeks and thus subverted the basis of Victorian Hellenism.[45] Plato claimed in the *Republic* that changes in music were associated with radical political change (*Republic* 424b–e) and studies of the performance history of classical receptions in opera have tended to bear this out.[46] At the Edinburgh International Festival in 2002 the staging of the opera *Oedipus Rex* by Stravinsky, directed by François Girard with the Canadian Opera Company and sung in Latin with English surtitles, was preceded by a performance of the Symphony of Psalms, accompanied by a video-wall recording the names of Aids victims and contextualizing for the audience the representation of the plague in the opera that followed.

Cultural Exchange

It is also the case that music, song, movement and acting styles have triggered debates about the validity or otherwise of cultural exchange in the staging of ancient drama. Arguments for 'authenticity' in language, setting and staging are very often complicated by the commercial realities of location and finance but deeper cultural issues are at stake. In 1996 Herbert Golder published an iconoclastic article[47] in which he expressed a deep disenchantment with almost all contemporary staging because he considered that modern resonances and acting styles were privileged over the Greek. His main conclusion was that 'the ephemeral must never be allowed to occlude the essential'. This of course encodes a particular view of 'the classical tradition' as a vehicle for transmission of a closed theatrical tradition rather than as a strand in the processes of reception and refiguration. Golder specifically rejected insights from other traditions, such as Japanese Noh drama in the context of his critique of 'avant-garde' productions such as Mnouchkine's *Les Atrides*, although interestingly he did state that he considered the gospel choir version of *Oedipus at Colonus* to be more faithful to ancient tradition. This was adapted as *The Gospel at Colonus*, an oratorio set in a black

[45] Goldhill (2002), 7.

[46] See especially Marianne McDonald, '*Medea è mobile*: the Many Faces of Medea in Opera' in E. Hall, F. Macintosh and O. Taplin (edd.), *Medea in Performance, 1500–2000* (Oxford, 2000), 100–18 and M. Ewans, *Wagner and Aeschylus: the Ring and the Oresteia* (London, 1982).

[47] H. Golder, 'Geek Tragedy? Why I'd rather go to the movies', *Arion*, third series 4.1 (Spring 1996), 174–209.

Pentecostal church service and staged by Lee Breuer from 1983–1988, including a Broadway run. Golder's reaction suggests that national and cultural conceptions of classicism (that is, cultural horizons that are familiar) are at the root of much debate concerning artistic merit and the appropriateness of the correspondences made with modern perceptions of ancient productions. Arguing against Golder's position there are a number of researchers and critics who point to the way in which interaction with non-western cultural traditions can bring back to ancient drama some of the elements which have been marginalized by western appropriations.[48]

These vigorous debates underline ways in which reception studies also have an important part to play in the reassessment and reconstruction of the interpretation, staging and cultural and political contexts of ancient drama. There are signs that a new kind of philology, a philology of reception, is being developed. This research includes tracking the migration routes of ancient texts through other theatrical and literary traditions. It also includes study of the verbal and non-verbal languages used in bringing texts to the stage and comparison of the contexts of creation and production, both ancient and modern.[49] When this new philology comes together more systematically it will provide a range of tools through which scholars can describe and analyse the relationship between ancient texts and their subsequent staging. This mapping of the commonalities and differences between ancient plays and their modern analogues is an essential pre-requisite to evaluative judgements about the receptions and their cultural impact.

---

[48] For discussion of the impact of non-western theatrical traditions on modern productions of Greek drama, see F. Macintosh in Easterling (1997) and Wiles (2000). For recuperation of lost elements, see L. Hardwick, 'Greek Drama and anti-colonialism: Decolonising Classics' in E. Hall, F. Macintosh and A. Wrigley (edd.) (Oxford, 2003), forthcoming.

[49] Important recent additions to this research are in P. Easterling and E. Hall (edd.), *Greek and Roman Actors: Aspects of an Ancient Profession* (Cambridge, 2002).

V. FILM AND POETRY

Film

The growth of film criticism in modern reception studies presents in a particularly acute form many of the issues of method with which other areas of reception are also grappling. In addition, it brings together under the umbrella of one art form the sometimes uneasy relationship between 'high' cultures and popular forms of entertainment. 'Spectacle' has to be analysed alongside that of the most nuanced 'avant-garde' production techniques. Film has been closely related to drama in terms of analytic approaches, not just because of its links with the subject matter of ancient texts but because it is, like theatre, a performative medium – although unlike a staged performance the conditions in which it is created both assume and facilitate its preservation. Yet some aspects of film also move close to poetry. Furthermore, film poems based on ancient texts and paradigms have encouraged a more self-referential approach, reflecting on the relationship between words and images in both public and private contexts of reception. It will become clear from the discussion which follows that film receptions have some significant overlaps with those in drama and poetry.

Film is a comparatively new area in reception research and the development of critical approaches and methods rigorously tailored to the medium are as yet embryonic. In this chapter I shall outline the most important ones and suggest directions in which they might, or should, develop. Classical reception and film studies also reveal in a particularly acute way the tensions between 'traditional' approaches and more radical forms of analysis.

In chapter 3 I referred extensively to the work of Maria Wyke on film in the context of classical appropriations by fascist and liberal ideologies. Her work has centred on two of the major cinematic traditions in the twentieth century, in Hollywood and in Italy. Wyke's ground-breaking book *Projecting the Past: Ancient Rome, Cinema and History*[1] focused on four examples of how episodes from ancient Roman culture were appropriated in order to address modern issues (Spartacus and the slave uprising; Cleopatra's threat to Rome and associated gender

---

[1] (New York and London, 1997).

stereotypes; persecutions and excess in the time of Nero; and film representation surrounding the destruction of Pompeii). Wyke's approach is primarily historicist and addresses mainly Roman material but her concluding chapter ('A Farewell to Antiquity') also considers the impact of box-office decline of the 'blockbuster' after the 1960s and the distaste felt by younger and more cinematically sophisticated audiences for outmoded narrative forms.

This shift was reflected in the prominence of European 'art house' films in the 1960s and early 1970s. Most of these films represented Greek material mainly from tragedy, but one in particular, *Fellini – Satyricon* directed by Federico Fellini (1969), took Petronius' satiric novel and used it to address central questions concerning the relationship between cinema and classics with, in this case, a focus on 'the value of cinema as a means of reconstructing and consuming ancient Rome in the present'.[2] The film's structure of a series of episodes without a coherent narrative link and its representation of Petronius' parody of mythic heroism used the wide frame of Cinemascope to emphasize successions of images rather than to narrate the development of characters or to communicate their point of view. Thus distinctions between 'reality' and 'illusion' became blurred. The alienation of the viewer was accentuated by dubbing which disrupted the association between the actors' lips and the dialogue and by a musical score based on electronically produced metallic sounds. This approach not only subverted the tradition of the epic film but also, according to the director, represented the way in which archaeology can reveal fragmented images of a vanished world, in this case caught unawares by modern cinematic techniques.

In order to address this kind of cinematic development, reception scholars have to take full account not only of the conditions of production (choice of subject, economic conditions of financing and marketing, impact of directors and actors and situation of the film in relation to their other work) but also of the formal and technical use of the medium and its redrawing of the possibilities of representation and communication. This kind of methodology has been quite slow to develop. The most influential approach has been imported into classical reception from Shakespeare studies and in particular via the work of Jack J. Jorgens.[3] Jorgens classified films of Shakespearean tragedy under three main headings:

---

[2] Wyke (1997), 188.
[3] Jack J. Jorgens, *Shakespeare on Film* (Bloomington, 1977).

(i) *theatrical mode* in which film was used as a recording device to try to capture what was essentially a theatrical performance;

(ii) *realistic mode* which moved away from an overtly theatrical setting to a naturalistic situation;

(iii) *filmic mode* in which the film maker or director makes full use of the medium's own forms and technology.

These categories were adapted for discussion of classical film by Kenneth MacKinnon.[4] MacKinnon added a fourth category, that of *metatragedy* to recognize the way in which films were increasingly not just reminding audiences about ancient works but also investigating their relationship with the modern film. MacKinnon clarified the categories by discussing specific examples for each. Under *theatrical mode* he included the earliest filmed record of a modern production of Greek drama, the vision-only eleven-minute extract from the 1927 production of *Prometheus in Chains*, staged at Epidauros as part of the 'Delphic Idea' or movement towards world peace, a concept developed by Angelos Sikelianos and his wife Eva Palmer. The film provides important evidence for the combination of archaizing costume and chorus movement, taken from painted pottery, and the impact of Isadora Duncan's contemporary techniques in dance. More recent examples of the *theatrical mode* include Tyrone Guthrie's *Oedipus Rex* (1956) and a number of films of different performances of Sophocles' *Electra*.

Under *realistic mode* Mackinnon cited Michael Cacoyannis' three films based on Euripides (*Electra* (1961), *The Trojan Woman* (1971), and *Iphigenia* (1976)) while under *filmic mode* he suggested the most modern-seeming examples such as Jules Dassin's *Phaedra* (1961) and Costas Ferris' 'art movie' *Prometheus, Second Person Singular* (1975). Under *metatragedy* Mackinnon placed Jules Dassin's *A Dream of Passion* (1978), which featured one of the stars playing Medea in a modern production, and Pasolini's *Oedipus Rex* (1967) which alluded to Pasolini's own biography and emphasized the importance of Freud's conception of the Oedipus Complex.[5]

MacKinnon's typology has continued to be extensively used as a basis

---

[4] K. MacKinnon, *Greek Tragedy into Film* (London, 1986).

[5] For further discussion of critical reaction to these films and their relationship with the ancient texts see Kenneth MacKinnon, 'Film Adaptation on the Myth of Textual Fidelity' in L. Hardwick (ed.), *Tony Harrison's Poetry, Drama and Film: the Classical Dimension*, The Open Colloquium 1999 (Milton Keynes, 2000), 16–28 and electronically at http://www.open.ac.uk/Arts/Colq99/MacFinal.htm.

Fig. 7 *After Homer*, ODC Theatre Company, Edinburgh and the Opera House of Cairo 2002, directed by Elli Papakonstantinou. Stathis Mermigis in a music and movement sequence based on Aiolos' bag of winds and the storms endured by Odysseus (*Odyssey* X). Photo: Nikos Andritsakis.

Fig. 8 Rudolph Walker as Blind Billy Blue, the jazz-playing bard, in the 1992 Royal Shakespeare Company production of Derek Walcott's *The Odyssey: a Stage Version*, directed by Gregory Doran. Photo: Mark Douet.

for analysing classical films because it provides a way of assessing the relationship between ancient text and classical film-as-genre without necessarily using that relationship as an arbitrary criterion of value. However, some more conservative critics have attempted to circumscribe the characterization of the classical film genre by suggesting that it must conform to a notion of classical 'status' framed by three elements – form (as characterized by Aristotle); imitation of classical models (formulated by one critic as 'classical theory insists upon the primacy of the original . . . the basic and fundamental elements must not be changed'); ahistoricity – 'knowledge is found in the general conclusions that have stood the test of time'.[6] Genre classification in film is more prevalent than in critical approaches to other art forms and does not attract the same criticisms for being outmoded. Nevertheless the definition of classical 'status' quoted above to some extent parallels that to be found in conservative approaches to other areas of reception studies, including translation.

In a vigorous article which both supports the contribution of genre studies to film and refutes ultra-traditionalist formulation of classicism, Mary-Kay Gamel[7] identified the importance for reception criticism of systematic comparison of ancient drama and modern film in terms of formal, thematic and affective features. She also noted that like drama, film is (despite the focus on the director and individual *auteur* theory in film) the product of a combination of talents of author, director, actors and musicians. Gamel has also argued that material aspects are crucial, including the origins of financial support for creation and distribution of the work. Ancient drama and modern film also share the potential of an appeal to a large and socially diverse audience. Gamel showed that an over-emphasis on filmic treatment undervalues the impact of the other aspects and that a full treatment, for film as for drama, must take account of all of them if the scope of the term 'text' is not to be fatally narrowed. She also reasserted that the concept of genre (e.g. epic, *film noir*, science fiction, westerns, war film, *avant garde*) is, like individual works, located within history and that any film must be considered in the context of its generic tradition. The presence or dominance of certain genres at a particular time and their absence at others are one index of

---

[6] Thomas Sobchack, 'Genre Film: a Classical Experience', first published in *Literature/Film Quarterly* 3 (1975), 196–204 and reprinted in Barry Keith Grant (ed.), *Film Genre Reader* (Austin, 1986); quoted and discussed by Mary-Kay Gamel, 'American Tragedy: *Chinatown*' in Martin M. Winkler (ed.), *Classics and Cinema*, Bucknell Review (1991), 209–31.

[7] Gamel (1991).

ideological change[8] as are the counter-texts snapping at the conventional frameworks of genres.

Also significant is the question of shifts of emphasis within a genre, for instance in selection of classical referents or the ways in which these are addressed. In his discussion of film treatment of Medea,[9] Ian Christie drew links between the categories of film representations, selectivity in respect of the ancient text, and the particular social and artistic expectations in respect of the genre made by the receiving society. He argued that Medea was avoided by film makers for a long time because her story did not fit in with the borrowings made by film from nineteenth-century stage traditions and other vernacular narrative media that combined sentiment with sensation. For example, moralizing and melodrama were popular in the early twentieth century yet the shocking demands of the Medea story exceeded the bounds of melodrama and did not offer the redemptive element required by the moralizing tradition. Only in what Christie called 'the permissive and experimental sixties' could the taboos surrounding what could be shown and seen be broken. In this respect cinema norms differ from those of Greek drama in which violence occurs off stage and is communicated through narrative. In film, events are shown rather than narrated and while the revenge killing of Glauce could be accommodated, the killing of the children could not.

Christie linked the transgressive elements of the 1960s with a new sense of the relationship between the political and the psychosexual. This was demonstrated in Pasolini's *Medea* and later developed in Jules Dassin's *A Dream of Passion* (1978) which was written and directed in Greece three years after the collapse of the military junta (the colonels' régime), against which both Dassin and his wife Melina Mercouri (who played one of the Medea figures in the film) had protested. Christie's approach also considers the ways in which filmic adaptations replace elements excluded by ancient authors or draw on other ancient sources. For example, Pasolini included Colchis and Medea's role as sorceress as a prelude to her domestication by Jason, while Dassin alludes to the reinterpretation of Euripides' play in the context of modern theatre performance and the contemporary environment of marital breakdown and child killing. Thus both receptions create a 'double perspective', encoding reflection on both Euripidean and modern refigurations. Like

[8] Gamel (1991), 226–7.
[9] I. Christie, 'Between Magic and Realism: Medea on Film', in E. Hall, F. Macintosh and O. Taplin (edd.), *Medea in Performance* (Oxford, 2000), 144–65.

Wyke and Gamel, Christie's approach also locates the films within the director's works as a whole, particularly in relation to the visual styles used in the films – for instance in the use of 'montage' to allow accumulation of meaning within and between images (as in Lars von Trier's Danish version of *Medea*, 1988) or in Pasolini's enigmatic discontinuity in camerawork. Christie also points to the way in which the development of psycho-analytic film criticism has linked the story of Medea to elements in modern horror films (crossing the border between human and monster, human and alien) and suggests that this involves a mutation of Medea into a Medusa figure.

Films which move away from ahistoricity, whether in setting or in subject matter, are usually engaged in some kind of mutation of myth. One notable example is the Colombian production *Edipo Alcalde* (Mayor Oedipus), 1996, a joint Colombian, Mexican and Spanish production directed by Jorge Ali Triana. Triana was the founder of the Popular Theatre of Bogota and subsequently became director at the National Theatre of Colombia and the Spanish Repertory Theatre in New York City. The screen-play for *Edipo Alcalde* was by Gabriel García Márquez (the Nobel Prize-winning novelist) and the film was chosen for the Directors' Fortnight at the Cannes Film Festival in 1996. The cast of Colombians was augmented by Cuban, Spanish and Mexican actors in the star roles. The film adapted Sophocles' *Oedipus the King* to tell the story of a young man (Edipo) sent by the government in the mid-twentieth century to a small town in the Andes Mountains to run the mayor's office in the face of the violence and hate felt by various factions in the town. On his way he is ambushed but escapes by killing his attackers. Later the body of a popular local political leader is discovered. The director, Triana, described the film as 'a primal cry from the heart against irrational violence in this Latin American country' and told how Gabriel García Márquez had always wanted to 'adapt the Greek classic to the Colombian reality'. The Mayor follows the Oedipal path to unwitting incest and only gradually, prompted by a blind old man who is constructing a coffin for him, comes to realize that he himself was the killer of the local leader. A popular review made the obvious deduction: 'The story is set in present-day war-torn Colombia, with the South American country's civil strife standing in for the Theban Plague'.[10]

In addition to its artistic merit and interest to film specialists generally

---

[10] *Variety*, 27th May, 1996.

(it was included in the season of Colombian cinema 'From Reality to Magic' at the National Film Theatre London in 2002), *Edipo Alcalde* is important in two respects for reception studies. Firstly, it is one of a number of recent examples which challenge the view that Sophocles' *Oedipus the King* is hardly ever rewritten or adapted.[11] The reasons generally given are that the myth is not easy to translate into modern situations because the intervention of Freud's theory narrows its scope to the psycho-analytic (and is thought therefore to preclude other resonances) or that since Sophocles' play is about social and personal responsibility it is not well attuned to the concerns of contemporary western culture. Actually, *Oedipus the King* was banned by the censors from the professional stage in Britain until 1910, so it could be argued that Freud's theory is, on the contrary, part of a liberating tendency.[12] When these claims are considered it becomes significant that the film *Edipo Alcalde* was made by an international cast which was prepared to cross psychological as well as cultural boundaries. Furthermore, other adaptations of Sophocles' play in the last fifty years have built on its potential to say the unsayable and explore culturally and politically dangerous or controversial material. Important examples include Ola Rotimi's play *The Gods are not to Blame* (1968) in which the play becomes an analogue for the intertribal fighting of Africa and especially the Biafran war. More recently, Rita Dove's *The Darker Face of the Earth* (published 1994, first performed at the Oregon Festival in 1996 and subsequently at the Royal National Theatre in London) set the story in an ante-bellum cotton plantation in the southern states of the USA and explored the institution of slavery as the source of pollution. Incest is replaced as a focus by miscegenation. Thus what has been regarded by Aristotle, Freud and Lévi-Strauss as a text of central cultural dominance, becomes the vehicle for challenging dominance. It becomes a metaphor for the fraught discovery of the guilt of enslavers and colonizers.[13]

Sophocles' *Oedipus the King* was also the springboard text for David Greig's *Oedipus* (2000). This play, as yet unpublished, was the first of three plays which was performed in sequence in Glasgow in 2000 by

---

[11] See Karelissa Hartigan, *Greek Tragedy on the American Stage: Ancient Drama in the Commercial Theater, 1882–1994* (Westport, CT and London, 1995), 148.

[12] F. Macintosh, 'Under the Blue Pencil: Greek Tragedy and the British Censor', *Dialogos* 2 (1995), 54–70.

[13] This play is currently being researched by Barbara Goff as part of a wider study, B. Goff and M. Simpson, *Black Dionysus: Greek Tragedy in African and African-American Literary Cultures*. I am grateful to her for allowing me access to her work in advance of its publication.

theatre babel, directed by Graham McLaren, as a result of a commission
to three leading Scottish playwrights to adapt classical texts in the light
of the flourishing of theatre arts in the years before and following
devolution and the re-convening of the Scottish Parliament after a gap
of almost 300 years.[14] Greig's was a highly politicized version of
Sophocles' play. Costume and setting suggested the India of the British
Raj. The Indian context and associated religious ritual distanced the
struggle for political change from modern time and place yet there was
contemporary impact in the themes of transfer of power and the
exposure of corruption and disease. The design suggested that the
sun was setting over a colonized city. Yet this never became a 'closed'
reading – both usurper and liberator spoke in Scots' accent and idiom
and the identification of Creon and Oedipus with the roles of usurper
and liberator fluctuated throughout the play. The setting and focus
reminded anyone who was so tempted that Scots, too, were leaders in
the expansion and organization of the British Empire and thus the play
resisted facile equation with the notion that post-devolution Scotland
was emerging from colonial rule. Yet both histories, of the Raj, of
devolution and the associated crises of identity, were there. As the
director Graham McLaren put it, 'Politically Scotland is changing and
with the millennium the world is changing. Now is the time to be
defining what it is to be, not just a Scot in Scotland but what it is to be
human in the world . . . Oedipus is as close to a universal text as you'll
get. It starts off with the simple mystery of who killed Laius but finishes
up by asking absolute questions about what it is to be human.'[15] Thus it
is clear from reception of *Oedipus the King* in theatre and film that
analogues of Sophocles' play cross back and forth between the boundaries of the psycho-analytical and the political and in the adaptation of
the myth in both art forms the setting introduces an important
interpretive category – that of space and location.

This aspect of film as a receiver and adapter of classical plays has been
analysed by Pantelis Michelakis.[16] Michelakis set out to show how a
focused analysis of landscapes in films which adapted Greek tragedy
would also shed light on wider aspects of the politicization of antiquity.
He pointed out how individual landscapes had been used to generate

[14] The other plays were Tom McGrath's *Electra* and Liz Lochhead's *Medea*.

[15] Source: interview by Steve Cramer, Programme Notes (2000).

[16] P. Michelakis, 'The Past as a Foreign Country? Greek Tragedy, Cinema and the Politics of
Space' in F. Budelmann and P. Michelakis (edd.), *Homer, Tragedy and Beyond: Essays in honour of
P.E. Easterling* (London, 2001), 241–57, including filmography.

often incompatible readings of various ideological positions. Following the approaches developed by Turner in his study of cinema as social practice[17] Michelakis' study focused on how landscapes in classically generated films could be considered as a source for the shaping of social and personal identities. He concluded that there were two main types of cinematic landscape used to shape perceptions of Greek tragedy. The first was landscape that appropriated and 'recycled' images of antiquity that are familiar from the surviving monuments and artefacts. Examples in this category included *Antigone* (1961) directed by George Tzavellas which used impressive stage sets of the city of Thebes and Creon's palace inspired by classical architecture and iconography. Tzavellas also used film of the Greek countryside which drew both on the association between performances of tragedy and rural areas such as Epidauros and on the Greek tradition of period dramas, a film genre of the late 1950s. Tzavellas aimed to restore an authentic context for the film and his conception of this was shaped by his perception of continuity between past and present. Also in this category, Michelakis placed Michael Cacoyannis' *Electra* (1962) which eschewed stage sets for a countryside setting which, according to the director, 'owes everything to that part of Greece today which appears timeless . . . Greek tragedy has no age'.[18] Cacoyannis also included a sequence shot at the palace of Mycenae to suggest that Electra's past, too, can be excavated, reconstructed and interpreted in different ways. This link between psychological and historical analysis was also evident in two film versions of *Oedipus the King* which were set in archaeological sites (both were shot in 1967, one at Dodona, directed by Philip Saville and one at Tiryns, directed by Oswald Derke). Michelakis also points out how the 1980s and 1990s filming of productions in ancient amphitheatres became a staple in educational and sometimes in mainstream films. The convention was 'sent up' in *Mighty Aphrodite* (1996, starring Woody Allen) in which 'authentic' production of *Oedipus Rex* in a Greek theatre in Sicily was juxtaposed with modern dialogue.

However, from the late 1960s films of Greek tragedy moved away from the norms of neo-classical theatre and, as was discussed above, the classical past began to be explored in more visually innovative ways. Michelakis distinguishes three types of landscape setting which embody this shift within the genre of classical films. The first is the desert,

---

[17] G. Turner, *Film as Social Practice* (London, 1993).
[18] Quoted and discussed in Michelakis (2001), 244.

deployed by Pasolini in his *Edipo Re* (1967) and *Medea* (1970), in which the mythological figures are first shown in primitive, barbaric and sometimes non-Greek open landscapes which signify the contrast between myth and the modern urban landscapes to which the unfolding of their stories bring them. The desert-type setting was also used by Cacoyannis (*Trojan Women,* 1971, and *Iphigenia,* 1976) to evoke the bleakness and suffering of Greece in the context of the military dictatorship (1967–1974). Michelakis' second category is that of forest – 'the cinematic forests of Greek tragedy range from the murky marshland of Denmark (von Trier's *Medea,* 1987) to the deciduous forests of New England (Amy Greenfield's *Antigone: Rites for the Dead,* 1990) or the tropical rainforests of Colombia (*Edipo Alcalde*)'.[19] The categories of desert and forest show how apparently natural spaces come to be filled with contests of politics and ideology. Michelakis' third 'landscape', the city, is used to frame these contests. Relations between the three spaces involve a concept of travelling, of crossing borders, which is a major aspect of many classical films. Michelakis also analyses the importance of this aspect in relation to Tony Harrison's film poem *Prometheus* (1998) which was shot on location in industrial areas across Europe. He points out that the landscapes explored in classical films are part of the environment of the spectators as well as of the film and can represent shifts in physical environment, psychological state and ideological perspective, all of which also shape perceptions of the ancient texts.

Harrison's *Prometheus* has been a major focus for debate, partly because of the subject matter and partly because it represents a sub-genre, that of the film-poem, of which Harrison has been the major exponent. The combination of film as a medium for moving images and verse forms, including those drawing on classical material, has been crucial for Harrison's engagement with the most shattering aspects of twentieth-century events. His work has drawn on the capacity of film to give a voice and an image to the silenced and unrepresented and uses the potential of film as an interventionist medium which might reach audiences different from those which would attend a Greek play. Here, however, the difference between popular and avant-garde film is crucial. Film-poems might well be said to fall into the latter category and miss popular audiences, although some have been specially developed for television. Harrison has also aimed to develop refigured hybrid forms of artistic expression in order to address the barbarities of the

---

[19] Michelakis (2001), 248.

twentieth century. This last aim was explicitly addressed in his film-poem *The Gaze of the Gorgon*[20] in which he commented:

> The *barbitos*, the ancient lyre,
> since the Kaiser's day
> is resting with barbed wire
> Bard's hands bleed when they play
> the score that fits an era's scream,
> the blood, the suffering, the loss.
> The twentieth-century theme
> is played on barbed-wire *barbitos*
> (Published text, 71)

It is this combination of verse, TV, film and suffering that communicates Harrison's conception of 'public poetry'. His work deals with public themes yet it is also received in what he has referred to as the 'shared intimacy' of the viewers sitting at home 'in their twos and threes'. The relationship between private and public is strengthened. The techniques that have made his use of classical referents accessible to those without a classical education include the demotic idioms in his versions (including colloquialisms and expletives), the use of metre and rhyme and repetitions to create a sense of orality rather than of a written text and direct appeals to the audience in terms of subject matter and setting, in order to engage their empathy. Harrison wrote in his preface to the published text of *Prometheus* that in cinematic mode, experiencing and feeling the rhythm of the shots was like responding to literature. The effect is to remove from his refiguration of classical sources any association with privilege – as Hermes bemoans in *Prometheus* (which has its initial setting in a Yorkshire mining village as the pit is about to be closed),

> How can Olympus stay intact
> if *poetry* comes to *Pontefract?*[21]

The role of the poetry is to comment on the images (rather than the role of the images being to illustrate the words).[22] In *Prometheus*, although there is a (silent) chorus and a structure of *rhêsis* and *agôn*, the theatrical

---

[20] Published text, T. Harrison, *The Gaze of the Gorgon* (Newcastle upon Tyne), 1992.

[21] Published text, T. Harrison, *Prometheus* (Newcastle upon Tyne, 1998), 23.

[22] For a discussion of this approach in relation to Harrison's film poems in general, see Peter Robinson, 'Facing up to the Unbearable: The Mythical Method in Tony Harrison's Film/Poems' in L. Hardwick (ed.), *Tony Harrison's Poetry, Drama and Film: the Classical Dimension*, Proceedings of the Open Colloquium 1999 (Milton Keynes, 2000), 29–43 and electronically at http://www.open.ac.uk/Arts/Colq99/robinson.htm.

mode is subordinate to the filmic and to the metatragic – the relationship
between ancient tragedy and modern film.[23]

In his preface to *Prometheus*, Harrison commented on this aspect
when discussing the redemptive potential of tragedy: 'The performed
suffering was old, the redemption contemporary'.[24] The additional
challenge represented by his concern with very recent events is whether
art can bring redemption to suffering which is immediate. Some critics
have judged that Harrison's apparent claim that art can address the
totality of contemporary and recent suffering is flawed. Keith Miller
wrote in the *Times Literary Supplement* (May 1999), 'There is an
arrogant tendency to conflate all of the big themes of the past 1000
years into one enormous supermyth: Orgreave to Auschwitz via
Dresden, all aboard! One specific problem about this is that it is frankly
offensive to imply that sacking someone is the same as butchering them
alongside their families'.

Harrison's verse-film linked Prometheus' gnawed liver to the fascist
eagle of genocide and the destruction of the lungs of the coal miners and
it was the miners, consumed by the flames like the miners in Zola's
Germinal, who constituted the metal from which the statue of Prometheus was cast. In contrast to Miller's view, Edith Hall characterized
the film as 'the most important artistic reaction to the fall of the British
working class as the twentieth century staggered to its close, a fall
symptomatic of the international collapse of the socialist dream. The
film also offers the most important adaptation of classical myth for a
radical political purpose for years'.[25] Hall also pointed out how
Harrison's film-poem shared with Theo Angelopoulos' film *Ulysses'
Gaze* (1995) the concept of a journey through areas of Eastern European disintegration and depictions of monumental civic statuary. Both
films used techniques which explored related themes in cross-chrono-
logical movement rather than through linear narrative.

Hall categorized Harrison's *Prometheus* as threnody. However, its use
of various landscape settings and subversion of conventional classical
settings and iconography also bring it closer to the filmic techniques
discussed by Michelakis. Above all, the film aims at a new kind of
redemptive effect in that it holds up a mirror to horror – in Robinson's
words 'the work . . . . Allows us to gaze at the Gorgon (to see the horrors

---

[23] See further L. Hardwick, *Translating Words, Translating Cultures* (London, 2000), ch.8.
[24] Harrison (1998), vi–vii.
[25] E. Hall, 'Tony Harrison's *Prometheus*: a View from the Left', *Arion* third series, vol. 10, no. 1
(spring/summer 2002).

clearly) without turning to stone. This is the achievement of the public poet . . . It is Tony Harrison's mythical method, the way his aspiration for a public poetry is informed by a Greek tragic vision – a process that, in its open-eyed humanism and its realignment of the public and the private is profoundly political'.[26]

The reception and refiguration of classical material in film therefore raises particular issues of analysis and method. Film has affinities with and contrasts to both drama and poetry. It raises particular problems about forms of reception that cross genres and about the impact (both aesthetic and material) of new art forms and technologies, ranging from blockbuster to avant-garde to film-poem. Film is one form of reception that can be exploited both by the powerful (nations, corporations) and for the oppressed (as an interventionist vehicle). It raises special challenges for professional classicists in that film is increasingly a medium through which members of the public have their initial perspectives on the ancient world shaped. It can thus be seen as in competition with scholarship as an influencing force. The challenge to reception studies will be to formulate ways of identifying and discussing cultural and historical differences in film in a way which not only recognizes the importance of film as an entrée to interest in the ancient world but also develops forms of critical analysis which address the shaping force of the medium and of its exponents. The critical approaches discussed in this chapter represent the beginnings of the rigorous analysis that will need to be developed.

Poetry

It would be marvellous to be able to devote a whole volume to receptions of classical poetry. It is a rich area for personal research and enjoyment, aided by the considerable amount of material available in translations, anthologies (both themed and chronological) and comparatively recently in collections based on receptions of a particular author (Homer, Virgil, Ovid, Horace, Seneca).[27] My focus here can therefore be rather different and I shall aim to identify and to discuss some

---

[26] Robinson (2000), 40.

[27] The Penguin Classics series on ancient poetry in English, for example, contains volumes on all these poets. For an historical overview, see E. Smith, *A Dictionary of Classical Reference in English Poetry* (Cambridge and Totawa, NJ, 1984). For a comprehensive anthology see A. Poole and J. Maule (edd.), *Oxford Book of Classical Verse in Translation* (Oxford, 1995).

examples of three main aspects of reception of poetry. These are: receptions which create a new and influential work of literature, thus involving literary hybridity on a grand scale; receptions which select episodes or figures from classical poetry and rework them, often across genres or with other changes of form – these are receptions based on *paradeigma*; receptions which explicitly challenge the interpretation and value attached to a particular classical text. All these variations within reception involve a commentary on the literary and artistic aspects of the source; all bring, too, their own distinctive perspective on the language and ideas of their own day; all are situated within a broader corpus of work by the receiving poet and interpreted by readers and critics within contexts which can vary from an immediate and personal response to an attempt to situate the work critically in past poetic traditions and current trends. It is a commonplace to point out that readers, unlike theatre audiences, may be sitting alone and that they have the opportunity to return to the texts in a way in which audiences cannot directly re-experience the performance. This allows first-stage reception, whether by the poet, the reader or the critic to become progressively more nuanced and sensitive to the impact of intertextuality at various stages of a poem's migration, both within antiquity and subsequently.

Receptions as new works

Even within the broad categories of poetic reception that I have identi-fied, there are considerable differences in relationship to the source text, in the development and variations in language and in the way in which critics and later poets have situated the 'new' work in its own tradition. For example, Gavin Douglas' translation into Scots of Virgil's *Aeneid* (published posthumously in 1553, although completed in 1513) was a pioneering work undertaken before the Renaissance had developed public taste for translations of Latin writers. This meant that he was less constrained by 'models' than those who, for example, translated Virgil after Dryden (1697) or Homer after Pope (*Iliad* 1715–20, *Odyssey* 1725–6). Although Chaucer had translated shorter passages, Douglas' was the first example of translation of the *Aeneid* into either Scots or English. Douglas' discussion of the problems of the translator (Prologue to Book 1) adopts a slightly deprecating attitude, suggesting that it is rough when compared to the Latin. Yet, paradoxically, translating classical texts was becoming a sign of linguistic vigour and cultural independence. Douglas also took on the role of critic, including short 'commentaries' on Virgil's characterization and images and aiming to make the work comprehensible to illiterate listeners and to school-children. He also made significant creative additions, especially in the passages which recount the relationship between Dido and Aeneas (Ezra Pound said that Douglas 'gets more out of Virgil than any other translator' – a tribute both to his scholarship and to his creativity). Linguistic analysis has shown that Douglas's new work also expanded the range of the Scots language and increased its flexibility in exchanging words between Scots and English. In the eighteenth- and twentieth-century literary revivals in Scotland his work became influential in his home country.[28]

The next major new work to take its inspiration from classical epic was George Chapman's *Iliad*. In his allegorical poem 'Euthymiae Raptus' ('The Tears of Peace', 1609) Chapman created a scene in which he encounters the ghost of Homer, setting his work within a tradition stretching from Dante's relationship with Virgil in *The Divine Comedy* to T.S. Eliot's representation of the 'familiar compound ghost' in 'Little Gidding' (1942, and as part of *The Four Quartets*, 1943). Chapman specifically referred to his sense that Homer was 'born in England : see him over-shine / All other country poets' ('The Reader', prefacing his translation of *The Iliad*). For Chapman, Homer was 'the first and best' and his translation was well received initially, although overshadowed by the Renaissance emphasis on Virgil and the eighteenth-century popu-larity of Pope. Chapman later provided inspiration for Keats (honoured in Keats's sonnet 'On first looking into Chapman's Homer' and thus leading indirectly to Elizabeth Cook's *Achilles*, 2001). However, later nineteenth-century critics such as Arnold thought Chapman's work over-complex while Swinburne considered Chapman to be a barbarian and lacking in Hellenism.[29]

Dryden's translation of Virgil's *Aeneid* (1697) also became an influential work in its own right, partly because of Dryden's role as a translator who commented on the art itself, partly because of his role as

---

[28] For current debates on Douglas's work, see A.E. Christa Canitz, 'In our Awyn Language: the Nationalist Agenda of Gavin Douglas "Eneados"', *Vergilius* (1996), 25–37 and M. Tudeau-Clayton, 'Richard Carew, William Shakespeare, and the Politics of Translating Virgil in Early Modern England and Scotland', *International Journal of the Classical Tradition*, vol. 5 no. 4 (Spring 1999), 507–27.

[29] For further discussion of the reception of Chapman, see Simeon Underwood, *English Translators of Homer from George Chapman to Christopher Logue* (London, 1998). Underwood usefully points out that the terms of Swinburne's criticism reveal more of Swinburne's Hellenism than of Chapman's.

'the English Virgil'. Dryden was thought to have raised English poetry to
new heights as well as recreating Virgil's poem in a way which was
equally attractive to those who knew the Latin and those who did not.
His poem was extensively excerpted in the commonplace books of
poetry that were influential in shaping eighteenth-century poetic tastes
and his admirers included Congreve, Pope, Gray, Byron, Burns,
Coleridge, Hopkins, Tennyson and Browning. In the first century
after his death, Dryden's translations (written in the 1690s) were
thought to be his greatest work. Only later were they neglected in
favour of his satirical and more obviously 'public' poetry of his earlier
work (such as *Absalom and Achitophel*).

Dryden's approach to translation is best known for his distinction
between three types of response to the source text.[30] These were
'metaphrase' (word by word and line by line), 'paraphrase' (keeping
the author 'in view' but following the words less strictly than the sense)
and 'imitation' (which Dryden described as 'forsaking' both words and
sense in favour of creative adaptation). Dryden was scathing about
metaphrase, which he likened to verbal copying ('Tis much like dancing
on ropes with fettered legs – a foolish task'). Imitation in his account
allowed the translator to become more visible but could do 'the greatest
wrong . . . to the memory and reputation of the dead'. He therefore
preferred paraphrase, although the dedication to his translation of the
Aeneid shows a further shift back towards a point between paraphrase
and literal translation, because of his wish not to lose Virgil's 'graces, the
most eminent of which are in the beauty of the words'. More recently,
Dryden's translation of Virgil has attracted renewed attention because of
the way his style absorbed the language of Spenser, Shakespeare and
Milton and because of his use of his translator predecessors. This
exemplifies the trend in reception studies to look at the interfaces
between aspects of the classical tradition itself and the other literary
forces present in a writer's work.[31]

This interface was also important in the critical reception of Alex-
ander Pope's versions of Homer. In his *Life of Pope* (1781) Dr. Johnson
praised the translations over and above Pope's 'original' works because
'His version may be said to have tuned the English tongue'. Yet the poet

---

[30] J Dryden, Preface to translation of *Ovid's Epistles* (1680).

[31] See especially C. Burrow, 'Virgils from Dante to Milton' in C. Martindale (ed.), *The Cambridge Companion to Virgil* (Cambridge, 1997), 79–90 and S.J. Harrison, 'Some Views of the *Aeneid* in the Twentieth Century' in S.J. Harrison (ed.), *Oxford Readings in Vergil's Aeneid* (Oxford, 1990), 1–20.

Cowper judged Pope's translations more cautiously on the grounds that they lack 'the air of antiquity' and were inaccurate (Cowper published his own translations of Homer in 1791). The history of composition of Pope's work is well documented.[32] Like Chapman, Pope used earlier commentaries and criticism and also considered the prose translation into French by Anne Dacier (1711). Although Pope's Greek was better than Chapman's he was largely self-taught and frequently consulted scholars. He also included an extensive commentary which situated Homer within the epic tradition of Virgil, Milton and Dryden as well as in relationship to the Bible. His commentaries synthesized rather than challenged earlier commentators and appropriated Homer into the epic tradition in English as its founder. Later there was further reaction against Pope's 'pseudo-poetic diction' (notably from Coleridge but also in a scholarly context epitomized by Bentley's aspersion that although Pope's *Iliad* was a very pretty poem, it was not Homer). Pope's use of the rhyming heroic couplet reflected the fashion of the time and perhaps partly accounts for later reactions against his version when the tastes of the Augustans became less popular.

The canonicity thus accorded to Homer and Virgil in the epic tradition of poetry in English has been both reinforced and challenged by the modern 'epic' Derek Walcott's *Omeros*.[33] This long poem is paradoxical in its stance towards the epic tradition. It is permeated by allusions to and echoes of Homer, Virgil and Dante and framed by the themes of imperialism and diaspora, yet it communicates these through the activities, images and direct speech vernacular of popular culture. It could not be described as a translation or even adaptation in any strict sense. (Walcott knows Latin but not Greek and claims not to have finished reading *The Odyssey*.) However, Walcott makes use of translational techniques such as names (Achille, Hektor, Helen) and refines the simile to suggest relationships between ancient and modern as well as to allegorize figures like History (with a Circe-like role). Walcott also uses classical paradigms, such as the *katabasis* or descent to the Underworld in order to revisit the African past of those who were transported to the Caribbean by slave-traders. The poem thus represents a new kind of epic which uses fragments or sherds from ancient culture but refigures them in a New-World context which acknowledges the power of the past but also recognizes that it cannot be recreated or relived.

[32] For a summary, see Underwood (1998), 33–7.
[33] D. Walcott, *Omeros* (London, 1990).

Walcott's work is central to a radical examination of two kinds of literary movement. Firstly, his appropriation of Homer reflects both the literary influence of classical epic and also Homer's modern decentring from western culture. Secondly, Walcott creates a post-colonial literature which is inter- cultural and recognizes both European and African traditions.[34]

Reception of paradigms

It is clear from the analysis of epic receptions of classical poetry that a provocative feature of the reception of ancient poetry is the recurrence of particular images or episodes often reworked in different forms and genres. Myths, legends and episodes have provided paradigms, that is, tales told and retold through individual works or successive texts providing models or contrasts either with other characters and events within the work or, more broadly, with the treatment of the same theme in other works. Significant examples within antiquity include the stories of Clytemnestra, Orestes and Electra and the themes of homecoming and recognition.[35] Poetic treatment of paradigms has to be distinguished from the distinctively Roman concept of *exempla* discussed in chapter 2. The comparatively straightforward emphasis on examples of conduct to be imitated or avoided is less specific in paradigm-based receptions (although it may be there). The stress is rather on re-examining recurrent motifs, sometimes in different contexts. For reception studies trends in the selection of particular paradigms may highlight shifts in perceptions of the relationship between ancient and modern.

Recent selections have included the episode of the killing of the suitors and hanging of the maids from *Odyssey* XXII. Derek Walcott's play *The Odyssey: a Stage Version* overturned the cultural power of the episode by making Penelope forbid the killing of the maid.[36] The episode has been violently reworked in Peter Reading's 'Homeric'[37] and by Michael Longley in 'The Butchers'.[38] Both poets follow closely the account in Homer but Longley elaborates the fumigation sequence to include an

---

[34] For detailed discussion see L. Hardwick (2000), ch. 6 'Walcott's *Philoctetes* : Imaging the Post-colonial tradition' and 'Reception as simile : the Poetics of Reversal in Homer and Derek Walcott', *International Journal of the Classical Tradition* vol. 3 (Winter 1997), 326–38.

[35] For detailed discussion of how poets treated such paradigms, see Jennifer R. March, *The Creative Poet*, ICS Bulletin Supplement 49 (London, 1987).

[36] Published text, D. Walcott, *The Odyssey: a Stage Version* (London, 1993).

[37] P Reading, *Collected Poems* 2 (Newcastle upon Tyne, 1996).

[38] M. Longley, *Gorse Fires* (London, 1991).

image of a priest exorcising the ghosts from the house, thus focusing both on the ghosts of the dead and on the affinities with Hermes who 'Like a clergyman might wave the supernatural baton'. Longley's work contains many examples of short poems in which he uses paradigms, usually from Homer, to make connections between ancient and modern and to re-examine the values of both – for example, in 'Eurycleia' (*Gorse Fires*, 1991) he uses the recognition scene and the boar's tusk scar on Odysseus' leg to introduce a simile between himself and Odysseus. The recognition scene as paradigm for exploration of human relationships is refashioned in 'Laertes' (*Gorse Fires*, 1991) while in 'The Helmet'[39] the scene between Hector and his baby son juxtaposes family love and the way that Hector

> Prayed that his son might grow up bloodier than him.[40]

One of the most influential images of war in Homer is included in the sequence on the shield of Achilles (*Iliad* XVIII). W.H. Auden's poem of the Shield of Achilles (in *The Shield of Achilles*, 1955) ruthlessly strips away the 'ritual pieties' and social cohesion expressed in Hephaistos' crafting of the shield and substitutes the execution of prisoners (or perhaps 'deserters'):

> (Barbed wire enclosed an arbitrary spot . . .
>   they were small
> And could not hope for help and no help came.)

Auden picks up the ambivalences in the Homeric rhetoric of war and explores these in a bleak image of large-scale suffering that is inclusive of both past and present:

> A plain without a feature, bare and brown
> . . .Yet congregated on its blankness, stood
> An unintelligible multitude,
> A million eyes, a million boots in line,

This self-conscious reflection on ancient poetics and the values which have been attached to it is a major feature of the work of Seamus Heaney. In his collection *Electric Light* (2001) Heaney explores the Latin Eclogue as a vehicle for addressing the poet's relationship to contem-

---

[39] M. Longley, *The Ghost Orchid* (London, 1995).

[40] For further discussion of Longley's receptions of Homer, see L. Hardwick 'Contemporary Receptions of Homer' in R. Fowler (ed.), *The Cambridge Handbook to Homer* (Cambridge, forthcoming, 2003).

porary events.[41] The exploration is poetically and personally self-conscious, based on a dialogue with the source and mediating poets who have used the form. In *Bann Valley Eclogue* Heaney's engagement with the tradition not only deploys the Latinate vocabulary found elsewhere in the collection but also directly examines the cultural impact of words from Virgil's *Fourth Eclogue*. Virgil himself is made to generate the discussion:

> Here are my words you'll have to find a place for:
> Carmen, ordo, nascitur, saeculum, gens
> Their gist in your tongue and province should be clear
> Even at this stage

Virgil's gently mocking comment introduces Heaney's re-working of these terms in the context of modern Ireland 'piety, order, the times / The nation, wrong and renewal, then an infant birth / And a flooding away of all the old miasma'. The figure of the poet in the poem refigures the 'messianic' birth of the child in Virgil's poem in the context of his own rural childhood and the expected birth. Classical allusion and form enable him to bridge the gap between public affairs (blood, pollution, the guilt of civil war) and private (rebirth, hope, the countryside). Virgil is directly addressed as his 'hedge-schoolmaster', an allusion to the role of the hedge schools in Irish cultural memory. The schools were a source of learning at the time when the penal laws in Ireland forbade an official education for Catholic children (1690–1795). The classical elements in this education were influential in the nationalist tradition – as Canon Sheehan was supposed to have said in the nineteenth century, 'The scholars took their sods of turf under their arms for school seats but every boy knew his Virgil and Horace and Homer as well as the last ballad about some rebel that was hanged'.[42] Heaney's work exemplifies a reception of classical poetry which engages with forms, vocabulary and the overlap and differences in ancient and modern semantic fields in order to address both personal emotions and public dilemmas. His work brings out the way in which receptions of poetry, like those of drama, depend both on a sense of difference from the source texts and exploit the shared aspects of human activities and experiences.

---

[41] S. Heaney, *Electric Light* (London, 2001).

[42] Quoted by W.B. Stanford, *Ireland and the Classical Tradition* (Dublin 1976), 76. For further discussion of hedge-schools see L. Hardwick (2000), ch. 5 'Translation and Cultural Politics: the Irish Dimension' and for analysis of Heaney's engagement with classical poetry see L. Hardwick, 'Seamus Heaney's Classical Ground', forthcoming article.

Shifting values

Carol Ann Duffy's poems take paradigms and elaborate or extend them, filling in gaps and silences and altering the direction of the gaze, as in 'Mrs Teiresias', 'Mrs Icarus', 'Penelope' and 'Eurydice' ('In fact, girls, I'd rather be dead').[43] In the twentieth century there have been larger and more radical subversions in which receptions have challenged particular emphases in classical poetry and its interpretation and have used classical paradigms to contest not only the values expressed in the ancient work but also the value put on them subsequently and their role in modern *paideia*. Examples of this type of reception are found in free translations and adaptations and in new poems. Important examples of the latter have shaped the reception and refiguration of conceptions of war and heroism, particularly in the poetry of the trenches of the First World War. Few of the poems involve direct translation (even at the freer end of the scale). Their impact derives partly from allusion and more especially from the reworking of themes from Homer and images from ancient cultures to create multiple layers of meaning.

The kind of direct allusion involved in the translating of a figure or image into the early twentieth-century context implies at least an outline acquaintance with classical and later literary culture on the part of the imagined readers. For example, Patrick Shaw-Stewart compared his situation with that of Achilles ('Achilles came to Troyland / And I to Chersonese') but there is also an allusion to John Keats' claim that he was in battle with Achilles in Shaw-Stewart's lines:

> Stand in the trench Achilles,
> Flame-capped, and shout for me.

The lines were written in the Gallipoli campaign of 1915 and situate Shaw-Stewart not just as aspiring to the status of a hero (and, furthermore, one who reflects on the justification for war) but also as aspiring to be a poet in the tradition of Keats.

As the carnage of war increased, Homeric allusions increasingly drew out the ambivalent or menacing resonances with classical poetry. Isaac Rosenberg's allusion in *August 1914* (written in 1916; Rosenberg was killed in 1918)) to the simile in *Iliad* 11.67–71 in which Trojans and Achaians cut one another down like two lines of reapers harvesting

---

[43] Carol Ann Duffy, *The World's Wife* (Basingstoke and Oxford, 1999).

wheat or barley, became an imagist expression of the violation of both nature and humanity:

> A burnt space through ripe fields
> A fair mouth's broken tooth[44]

This image has direct impact for those who know no Homer. For those who do, the image brings out the horror latent in Homer, although it is Homer and not Rosenberg who shows that the reapers/killers are working on behalf of the rich and powerful.

More specifically didactic was the insistence of Wilfred Owen (killed 1918), in 'Dulce et decorum est' that the Latin tag 'Dulce et decorum est pro patria mori' (Horace, *Odes* 3.2.13) represented an 'old lie', used to delude the young into thinking that death in battle was glorious. The poem is a vicious attack, both on complacency and ignorance about the war in the home country and also on the use of *exempla* from the past to justify present values.[45] More subtle is Owen's poem *Strange Meeting* (1918) which is constructed round a *katabasis* or descent to the under-world which featured in Homer, Virgil and Dante as a stage in moral and spiritual enlightenment. Owen uses a variant of the epic device of *aristeia*, in which heroes demonstrated their courage and military skill, to bring about a reversal at the end of the poem in which it becomes clear that the 'narrator' himself has been killed and that in his encounter with the dead German, polarization of the ideas of friend/enemy and courage/wisdom is being challenged.[46]

Owen's challenges were to ignorance of the realities of war and to unthinking acceptance of precepts drawn from appropriated classical works. His refigurations themselves in fact draw closely on classical poetics. A very different approach to subverting the values associated with battle is taken by Christopher Logue in his Accounts of Homer. The term Account is used by Logue to distinguish his work from a translation or version. The multiplicity of meaning of the word Account both draws attention to his narrative approach and suggests that his is holding Homer to a reckoning. Logue's *War Music* (2001) draws on Books I–IV and XVI–XIX of the *Iliad*. Logue has served in the army and

---

[44] I. Rosenberg, *The Collected Works of Isaac Rosenberg: Poetry, Prose, Letters, Paintings and Drawings*, ed. I. Parsons (London, 1979).

[45] For further discussion of the poetic traditions drawn on, see Hardwick (2000), ch. 3.

[46] Owen's poem may also have drawn on his own experiences. In World War Two a Russian platoon commander recalled, 'When I killed a German with a knife for the first time, I saw him in my dreams for three weeks afterwards'. Personal testimony, quoted in A. Beevor, *Stalingrad* (London, 1998 and 1999), 288.

his other works contain poems exploring and challenging jingoistic approaches to war.

Three features of Logue's Accounts are of particular significance. The first is that he does not read Greek and began his work on the *Iliad* by studying translations by Chapman (1611), Pope (1720), Lord Derby (1865), A.T. Murray (1924) and E.V. Rieu (prose, 1950). His view was that in those writers, poetic value and knowledge of Greek were in inverse proportions and that there were as many Homers as there were translations.[47] The second important feature is that Logue developed a poetics very different from Homer's – he omitted formulaic epithets, truncated similes and tried to keep the action moving energetically forward by capturing key moments, often by using sharp commands or comments or introducing cinematic techniques into the poetry.[48] Thirdly, in both figurative language and description Logue drew out the dark side of Homer or replenished gaps in Homer. The ruthless and unquestioned exploitation of the women and the ordinary people which underlies Homer is never glossed over and the idea of reciprocity which is so sensitively shaded in Owen's and Longley's receptions is reduced to basic material exchange. Logue's Accounts not only undermine the concept of heroic values, they also challenge the value of Homer in that the emotional and moral sensitivity of the poetry of Books 6, 9 and 24 of the *Iliad* is by-passed.

This 'desanitizing' of Homer has provoked vigorous critical reaction. Some critics have pointed to the power of Logue's writing, its spareness and its cumulative effect. Others have emphasized the violence and cruelty which is communicated through Logue's adaptation of popular art forms. Logue's intervention is certainly revolutionary in terms of Homer reception and challenges the way in which Homer has been appropriated and interpreted in many aspects of the classical tradition.

The effect of those radical subversions of the paradigms of classical poetry is one of 'saying the unsayable', both in terms of critique of iconic appropriations and of confronting the suffering brought by war. In his introduction to *The Oxford Book of Modern Verse* (1936), W.B. Yeats explained why he had decided not to include any work by Owen, Sassoon, Graves and other war poets: 'they made suffering their own. I have rejected these poems for the same reason that made Arnold

---

[47] C. Logue, Introduction to *War Music* (London, 1981), vii.
[48] For detailed discussion of Logue's techniques, see Hardwick (2000), 56–61.

withdraw his *Empedocles on Etna* from circulation; passive suffering is not a theme for poetry . . . In all the great tragedies, tragedy is a joy to the man who dies; in Greece the tragic chorus danced . . . If war is necessary, or necessary in our time and place, it is best to forget its suffering as we do the discomforts of fever, remembering our comfort at midnight when our temperature fell'. Apart from the debatable generalization about Greek tragedy, two points in Yeats's reasoning stand out. The first is that 'passive' suffering, as opposed to *aristeia,* can be dismissed from poetry. The second is the implication that poetry cannot engage with suffering on the scale of that endured in the First World War. The War Poets directly countered both points by redefining the concept of the hero and challenging the heroic concept of the 'good death' (a death met with individual courage and which enabled the dead man to avoid the indignities of defeat, old age and decrepitude).

Yeats's doubts about the ability of poetry to cope with the enormity of suffering on a grand scale were refined in the comment of Adorno that there could be no poetry after Auschwitz. Both were challenged by the attempts of Tony Harrison in the film-poem *Prometheus* to encapsulate within the Prometheus myth the sufferings of twentieth-century Europe, including the bombing of Dresden, the Holocaust and the atrocities in the Balkans.[49] In Harrison's view, not only the ancient Greeks but also modern consciousnesses are tested to the limit in coping with catastrophe.

Harrison specifically addressed this in *The Labourers of Herakles*[50] in which he himself played the spirit of Phrynichus and spoke of 'redeeming destruction through the power of art' (text, 143). The allusion to Phrynichus brings into the argument the Athenian tragedian who wrote at the turn of the sixth and fifth centuries BCE and based some of his work on recent historical events rather than purely mythological material. It was a play on a contemporary theme, the *Capture of Miletus*, which led to his being fined for reminding the Athenians of their own troubles. Polarization of the concepts of poetry as catharsis and of poetry as a call to awakening is not confined to Aristotle. Auden, Owen, Longley, Logue and Harrison all develop the latter aspect in their own ways and in so doing redeem poetry from Homer onwards from charges of

---

[49] See further Hardwick (2000), 134–5.
[50] The play was performed in 1995. Published text, T. Harrison, *Plays* 3: including *The Labourers of Herakles* (London, 1996).

sanitizing suffering and its causes and of being appropriated for a modern *paideia* that includes the uncritical acculturation of war. In so doing they also strike a balance between exposing the alien qualities and contexts of classical poetry and building on the commonalities of suffering shared by other times and cultures.

VI. (RE)EVALUATIONS – (WHY) DO RECEPTION STUDIES MATTER?

There has been a paradox at the centre of much of the discussion in this book. On the one hand much of the material analysed and the issues raised have been shown to be central to public, artistic, political and cultural processes. In some cases (e.g. chapter 3) there has been direct tension between appropriation of classical referents for political or social purposes and the demands of the independence and integrity of scholarship. Related tensions may also arise when appropriation has commercial rationales. Educational appropriation, too, is selective and may have a strongly instrumental focus. On the other hand, I have urged caution in the face of the idea that the arts have a decisive function as shapers or transformers of consciousness although they are a constituent part of broader social and cultural fabrics. Accordingly, I have suggested that there are necessary distinctions to be made between the heightening of sensitivity or awareness on the part of individuals or groups who 'receive' and the translations of this awareness into considered action (whether personal, social or political). I have tried to show that any kind of appropriation for instrumental effect is necessarily two-edged and needs to be subject to the kind of scrutiny which identifies both commonalities and differences between the source text and the refigured text and which subjects both to contextual analysis and to investigation of the silences and marginalia embedded within them.

Running through this discussion have been two underlying trends. The first is that classical referents are still a vital springboard in new creative work. The second is that among the motivations of the receivers (whether artists, scholars, remakers or audiences) appreciation and enjoyment together form one of the important criteria by which the value of the classical referents may be judged. This of course raises further questions about the aesthetics, psychology and behaviours associated with enjoyment (which I interpret as experience, appreciation and pleasure in respect of the classical referent and its subsequent vitality).

In this final chapter, therefore, I want to try to get to grips with some key questions about why and how reception of classical texts and images can be shown to matter. It is necessary to probe evidence about possible practical implications for cultural change while avoiding the pitfalls of either appearing to accept trivial correspondences as 'influences' or subsuming in a woolly 'universalist' way all explorations of the human situation under a notion of unchanging human behaviour. It also has to be made clear that claiming the continuing importance of classical texts is not the same as attaching to them new kinds of foundation myths (which would have the potential for sinister results discussed in chapter 3).

The first part of this chapter examines examples of the kind of links which may be said to exist between exposure to classical refigurations and subsequent reflection and behaviour. The second identifies and examines different kinds of cultural processes which are involved in reception and considers the extent to which perceptions and practices coalesce. Thirdly, I shall go on to consider the place of reception study and practice in the construction of concepts of identity, both ancient and modern, with some attention to the effect which reception studies are beginning to have on perceptions of the characteristics and qualities of the ancient texts themselves (*their* 'identity', to extend the metaphor).

Making a difference to perceptions of life possibilities – the personal, the hopeful, the social

My first example is unashamedly atypical. In his memoirs *Long Walk to Freedom*[1] the former President of South Africa, Nelson Mandela, refers to various experiences which helped to create the beginnings of hope in his long imprisonment on Robben Island under the apartheid régime (Part 9, 'Beginning to Hope'). These included being allowed to leave cells for Sunday services ('during the first two years on the island, we were not allowed to leave our cells even for Sunday services. The minister would preach from the head of our corridor. By the third year, services were held in the courtyard', 536); sometimes the prisoners were allowed to organize a Christmas performance by what Mandela describes as 'our amateur drama society'. He continues with some irony 'our productions were what might now be called minimalist: no stage, no scenery, no costumes. All we had was the text of the play' (540). Mandela took part in a few performances during his 27 years in prison and recalls that he had one memorable role, that of Creon in Sophocles' *Antigone*. He had read a number of Greek plays in prison and 'found

[1] N. Mandela, *Long Walk To Freedom* (London, 1994 and 1995).

them enormously elevating. What I took out of them was that character
was measured by facing up to difficult situations and that a hero was a
man who would not break down even under the most trying circumstances' (p. 540). It is easy to see the attraction of the stance of Antigone
in that respect: 'It was Antigone who symbolized our struggle. She was,
in her own way, a freedom fighter, for she defied the law on the ground
that it was unjust'.

This aspect of the play was later prominent in the staging of *The
Island*, a collaboration between Athol Fugard, Winston Ntshona and
John Kani, first performed in 1973. The play became an icon for its
denunciation of the brutality and injustice of the apartheid régime.
Sophocles' *Antigone* had earlier been performed by the Serpent
Players, a group of black actors closely associated with the actor,
poet and playwright Athol Fugard and based in New Brighton (a
township outside Port Elizabeth). A performance of *Antigone* had to
be cancelled in 1965 because the actor Norman Ntshinga, who was to
play Haemon, was imprisoned on Robben Island for political activities.
The Island was not only a good example of a theatre workshop
production of township plays with co-operation across racial divides,
it was also historically specific in that the 'play within a play' drew on
the performance of *Antigone* by prisoners in which Nelson Mandela
participated.[2]

In *The Island* Winston is reluctant to dress up as a woman to play the
part of Antigone and his necklace made of nails, his wig made of string
and his false breasts intensify his embarrassment. However, the other
actor, John, consoles him, 'There'll come a time when they'll stop
laughing and that will be the time when our Antigone hits them with
her words' (*The Island*, Scene two). In performance (Scene four) the
play culminates in a *coup de théâtre* when Winston/Antigone tears off his
wig and false breasts and cries out 'Time waits no longer. I go now to my
living death because I honoured those things to which honour belongs'.
The two prisoners then resume the mime of shackled back-breaking
work with which the play began.

The Island was effective in enacting the dignity, even under degrading

---

[2] For discussion of the multiracial workshop tradition in South African drama, including
refiguration of classical plays, see Margaret Mezzabotta, 'Ancient Greek Drama in the New
South Africa' in L. Hardwick *et al.* (edd.), *Theatre Ancient and Modern* (Milton Keynes, 2000),
246–68, and also at http://www.open.ac.uk/Arts/CC99/mezza.htm. A related development is the
preparation of a new translation of Homer's *Iliad* by Richard Whitaker (University of Capetown).
The translation actively exploits synergy between Greek concepts and the semantic fields of the
languages of the modern South Africa.

treatment, of anti-apartheid protesters and in influencing liberal opinion in South Africa and abroad.[3] Yet it is equally significant for the purposes of this discussion that Nelson Mandela has emphasized the importance for him of playing the role of Creon: 'At the outset, Creon is sincere and patriotic, and there is wisdom in his early speeches when he suggests that experience is the foundation of leadership and that obligations to the people take precedence over loyalty to an individual . . . But Creon deals with his enemies mercilessly . . . His inflexibility and blindness ill become a leader, for a leader must temper justice with mercy' (541). Here, it is not Antigone who is a decisive icon, but rather the reflection on the role of Creon. It is as though the experience of playing Creon was a catalyst for Mandela's meditation on the requirements of leadership and conflict resolution. This is no monolithic seizure of Greek drama as 'example' but rather a process of personal development triggered by reflection on the dynamics of the play. And no-one could deny the indirect effects on the history of the new South Africa, reflected for example, in the establishment of the Truth and Reconciliation Commission.[4]

Antigone, despite the grim ending of the play, has frequently recurred in the context of hope and has been singled out as a text which evokes response in young people. The play was chosen as a key text by TAG Theatre Company (Theatre About Glasgow) in order to promote debate about personal responsibility in wider social contexts. The initiative was part of the *Making the Nation* 1999–2002 programme (part funded by the Scottish Arts Council and Glasgow City Council) which was a four-year participatory drama and theatre project developed in the context of Scottish Devolution and the reconvening of the Scottish Parliament in Edinburgh in 1999. The *Making the Nation* project included stimuli to debate the concepts of nationhood, democracy, government and collective and personal responsibility. It was launched at a special event in the new Museum of Scotland on 2nd March 1999. TAG, as Scotland's National Theatre for young people, wanted the project to contribute to Scotland's democratic renewal by 'providing a conduit for young people to explore national identities, to discuss their aspirations for their community and for Scotland'.[5] The artistic director for TAG, James Brining, set out the reasons for his choice of *Antigone*: 'I'm interested in

---

[3] For further discussion see Mezzabotta (2000) and D. Walder 'Resituating Fugard: South African drama as witness', *New Theatre Quarterly* 8/32 (November 1992), 343–61.
[4] For details of the Commission, see www.truth.org.za.
[5] Source: TAG Theatre Company Information Sheet.

young people, or audiences, whoever, asking questions about what it means to be a member of a society, of a community. Where does our responsibility begin and end? And that's something that is in the play. Where are the links between us?'.[6]

TAG Theatre Company therefore commissioned Sarah Woods, writer-in-residence at the Royal National Theatre, to produce a version of the play resonant with the concept of the *Making the Nation* project (the text was in 2002 still unpublished). This directly politically motivated refiguration has as its principal focus the exploration of the social reaction to Antigone's resistance to Creon's edict. Alison Burke's study of the play text and its performance and reception[7] focuses on the treatment of the chorus and the way in which it gradually moves from its position of neutrality to a position of support for Antigone's actions. In the process, the play challenges political apathy and questions the justice of violating the politically active individual. Burke's discussion also demonstrates how Woods's text, both as written and as performed, differs from Sophocles' play in that the audience is not asked to adjudicate between Antigone and Creon or to consider whether Antigone is right to insist on burial for her brother and if so, what are the justifying reasons. Instead, the focus is on the reaction of a community to the challenge presented by an individual. The set design and costume made some allusions to British imperial power and colonization (in relation to India and to Scottish participation in the military and political hierarchy) but these were suggestions; the production was not given a specific historical or geographical location. Although the play was generally well received by audiences, review critics questioned whether its focus was too political and whether it would actually strike a chord in the experience of young people. There is no evidence either for or against the proposition that the play would encourage debate about social and political action. Nevertheless, the project was based on the view that awareness of and reflection about the issues raised in classical plays would constitute a valuable part of the *paideia* or cultural framework that would equip young people for the future.[8]

---

[6] Source: James Brining interview with Rob Adams, *The Herald*, 29th August 2000, 18, quoted more extensively and discussed in Alison Burke, 'Totalitarianism, Martyrdom and Social Resistance : Sarah Wood's *Antigone*', *International Journal of Scottish Theatre* vol. 2 no. 1 (September 2001), 26pp, http://arts.qmuc.ac.uk/ijost/Volume1_no3.

[7] Burke (2001).

[8] The value of classical texts in debates of this kind was considered by the Appeal Court Judge, Sir John Laws, in 'The Margaret Howard Memorial Lecture on Law and Literature' (Oxford, 2002). An extract was printed in *Ad Familiares*, vol. xxiii (2002), xv–xvi.

The potential of *Antigone* for stimulating debate among young people also underlay the refiguration *Odàle's Choice* by Kamau Brathwaite, first performed at the Mfantisman Secondary School, Saltpond, Ghana in 1962.[9] Brathwaite had 'returned' to Africa from the Caribbean and was a government education officer in newly independent Ghana. The published text appeared in the series 'Plays for African Schools'. In the introduction the editor specifically draws out the play's relationship to Sophocles: 'it is modernised (though to an indefinite period) and made to apply to an African Country, but no country in particular . . . as the title implies [*Odale's Choice*] is the decision of the chief character, first to defy the wishes and instructions of her powerful uncle and, secondly, to refuse as a matter of principle the mercy he extends to her at the climax of the play'. The introduction also suggests that in order not to detract from the strength of the drama and the audience response, scenery and properties should be kept very simple and that this is best achieved by theatre in the round, rather than a stage. There is a Chorus of Women in the play but unlike Woods's chorus they do not express views other than to request mercy for Odale; their main function is first to sing a dance of praise for Creon. This leaves a greater role to the spectators in developing their own response. Again, there is no direct evidence of the play's effect on young people although its theatrical success is indicated by subsequent revivals. The play was later staged in Kenya and Nigeria and was also performed by the Trinidad Theatre Workshop in 1973, directed by Derek Walcott. The popularity of *Antigone* in *paideia* projects of this kind shows the capacity of ancient drama for adaptation in different historical and cultural contexts and its potential for suggesting equivalences with a variety of modern situations.

A rather different example of the possible impact of refiguration of ancient drama on modern audiences is that of Seamus Heaney's *The Cure at Troy: a version of Sophocles' Philoctetes* (1990, first performed in Derry, Ireland).[10] The play has provoked considerable debate about the representation of equivalence between ancient and modern situations. *The Cure at Troy* is framed by the image of Philoctetes' raw wound and a mounting sense of destiny and dread. The core of Heaney's translational technique is to use the Greek conventions, and especially the chorus, to move the action into the consciousness of the receiving audience.

---

[9] Published text, K. Brathwaite, *Odale's Choice* (London, 1967, reprinted 1993).
[10] Published text, S. Heaney, *The Cure at Troy* (London, 1990).

Sophocles' *Philoctetes* has been a rich source of adaptation in political contexts, for example in Heiner Müller's version *Philoktet* in the situation of the German Democratic Republic (former East Germany). It was first performed in 1968 in Munich in West Germany and not until 1977 in East Berlin (although a student performance took place in Leipzig in 1974). Müller's adaptation was initially interpreted as an allegory applying the Greek myth to Stalinism but in fact he made considerable change from the Sophocles.[11]

In contrast Heaney's version, especially in the printed text, is remarkably close to Sophocles in structure and content. The play is subtitled 'after *Philoctetes* by Sophocles'. The description 'after' indicates two kinds of relationship with Sophocles. Firstly, Heaney's play does follow Sophocles' narrative outline and centres on the imagery of Philoctetes' wound, with its pain, poison, decay and psychological effects. Heaney uses the Greek conventions associated with tragedy, especially in his retention of the role of the chorus, which he makes an interpreter, commentator and moral guide on the implications of the action. Heaney also replicates the Greek formal elements which were central to tragedy, especially the *agon* or debate between major characters and the *stichomythia* or sharp line-by-line exchange. He also communicates the intensive and sometimes problematic urgency of ethical choice.

However, the play is also 'after Sophocles' in the sense that in performance and reading it is filtered through the poets', actors', directors' and spectators' consciousness of the events of the late twentieth century and these become more important than the production conditions in Athens in the fifth century BCE. The balance between ancient and modern has been signalled visually in different ways by various directors – at the Lyric Players Theatre, Belfast in October 1990 the play's ambivalent relationship to modern perceptions of ancient culture was emphasized by the device of a white sheet which initially covered everything on the stage and then billowed up to reveal the fragmented head of a white classical sculpture. In contrast, a later production performed in a studio theatre in Edinburgh and at the Oxford Playhouse in 1999 put the emphasis from the beginning on modern resonances with the opening sequence staged as a student bar argument. The bar stools were later used as stepping stones across

---

[11] See further L. Hardwick, *Translating Words, Translating Cultures* (London, 2000), ch. 4.

which the characters carefully exited, an allusion, perhaps to an image favoured by Heaney in his lyric poetry.

Debates about whether (and if so, how) Heaney's play represents precise figures in the unionist or the Nationalist communities in the North of Ireland seem to me to limit the scope of the emotions and attitudes with which the play deals. Rather, it is in the chorus's Odes that Heaney departs from the usual lyric and religious registers of the Greek Chorus in order to articulate specific resonances for the contemporary situation in Ireland. Two of these Odes have become well known outside those who have read the text or seen the play performed. One demonstrates Heaney's wish to introduce modern analogies of the suffering inflicted on both communities:

> A hunger striker's father
> stands in the graveyard dumb
> The police widow in veils
> Faints at the funeral home
> (*The Cure at Troy*, 77)

Heaney noted in the Programme Notes for the production at the Tricycle Theatre, Kilburn in 1991 that he had written the play in verse 'in order to preserve something of the formal ritualistic quality of the Greek theatrical experience' but had also 'felt free to compose a number of new lines for the Chorus'. This anachronism has been found by some critics to be intrusive and Heaney later doubted its aesthetic value, 'considering that it reduced tension / like a puncture in a wheel'.[12] The other well-known instance of the words of the chorus in *The Cure at Troy* has achieved even wider discussion:

> History says, *Don't hope*
> *On this side of the grave.*
> But then, once in a lifetime
> The longed-for tidal wave
> Of justice can rise up,
> And hope and history rhyme.
>
> So hope for a great sea-change
> On the far side of revenge.
> Believe that a further shore
> Is reachable from here.
> (*The Cure at Troy*, 77)

---

[12] See the discussion in S. E. Wilmer, 'Seamus Heaney and the tragedy of stasis' in S. Patsalidis and E. Sakellaridou (edd.), (*Dis*)*placing Classical Greek Theatre* (Thessaloniki, 1999), 221–31.

'When hope and history rhyme' became a slogan taken up by newspaper headlines at the time of the Good Friday Agreement (Belfast 1998) but well before that the lines had taken on a public status when quoted in full by Mary Robinson, the newly elected President of the Irish Republic for 1990–1997, in her inauguration speech. In his study 'Seamus Heaney, Colonialism and the Cure'[13] Hugh Denard discusses how the lines established a continuing place in public rhetoric when they were repeated by the President of the United States, Bill Clinton, in a speech given on the steps of the Bank of Ireland (1st December, 1995) while on a visit to support the peace process. Denard points out the symbolism of the occasion since the Bank of Ireland still displays the iconography of Royal authority from its days as the Irish Houses of Commons and Lords under British Rule and faces the front gates of Trinity College, which was established in 1592 by Elizabeth I to be the educational support for the Anglicization of Ireland. Also in 1995, Jacques Santer, the President of the European Commission, gave an address to the Forum for Peace and Reconciliation in Dublin Castle. He also quoted from *The Cure at Troy* to express his aspiration that 'history and hope can be made to rhyme'. The Chair of the Forum, Judge Catherine McGuiness wrote in the *Irish Times* of her hope that 'these words could be a motto for the forum'. Denard's article goes on to argue the radical thesis that Heaney's version of *Philoctetes* actually challenges discourses that lock Catholics and Protestants in Ireland into accepting apparently historically determined roles as colonized and colonist, expressed through a continuing rhetoric of victim and oppressor and that in its redemption of Philoctetes' suffering *The Cure at Troy* actually offered early insights which were eventually incorporated into the institutions set up by the Good Friday Agreement and ratified by referenda both in the North and in the Republic: 'To that extent, *The Cure at Troy* both represents, and is *itself*, symbolically, a ground-breaking, post-colonial voice'.[14]

Of course, the adoption of words from a refiguration of Greek drama into public discourse on the Peace Process is not a simple transplantation. It owes much to the status of Heaney himself (later in 1995 to be awarded the Nobel Prize for Literature) and to public knowledge of his internal exile within Ireland. However, it does show that refiguration of classical texts can have a public role and can be one factor in a wider

---

[13] H. Denard, 'Seamus Heaney, Colonialism and the Cure', *PAJ : A journal of Performance and Art* 22.3 (2000), 1–18.
[14] Denard (2000), 2

cultural (and in this case political) process. It unites the personal, the hopeful, the social aspects of the 'making a difference' category with which this Chapter began and also opens up discussion of the broader cultural processes involved in different kinds of reception.

Reception and cultural processes

In the course of this Survey it has been shown that reception not only studies a wide range of cultural processes but also contributes to them, both directly and indirectly. Of these cultural processes the most significant are:

- The operations of various kinds of tradition that focus on the handing down or transmission of material from one generation to the next, sometimes through forms, conventions and scholarship which seek to transmit the 'essential' or 'real' classical original. Examples would include the attempted reconstruction of an ancient performance of tragedy or of the original language text of a poem, perhaps with commentary or interpretation. In the context of reception studies, too, these are valuable activities because they contain at least an attempt to identify (and sometimes detach?) the accretions which have subsequently become attached to, and embedded in, later perceptions of the ancient texts. This is not to say that it is ever possible to return to 'the text as it really was'. Even if a text can be plausibly reconstructed, the audience cannot; and if, inevitably, we read the past through a filter of receptions then, as Charles Martindale has argued, there are real doubts about whether the ancient meanings and contexts can ever be plausibly reconstructed.[15] But even if the relationship between filters of reception and perceptions of the ancient text is problematic, attempts to map and peel away layers of reception can be a valuable gadfly, both in the scholarship offered and in destabilizing easy assumptions about meaning (the reverse service, which shows how various receptions can illuminate the source text and its context, is also significant).
- The interaction of (classical) traditions with others. This kind of interaction may be intentional and perceived at the time or it may only be recognized in any detail afterwards (perhaps as result of reception scholarship!). Modern examples here would include *Odale's Choice*,

---

[15] C. Martindale, *Redeeming the Text: Latin Poetry and the Hermeneutics of Reception* (Cambridge, 1993).

the adaptation of Sophocles' *Antigone* in an African context by
Kamau Brathwaite discussed above and especially the intermingling
of Greek and African approaches to the celebratory and lamenting
functions of the chorus. In this category might also be included the
choreography and emotion represented by various kinds of dance and
movement traditions. Examples include Jazz Art in South Africa, as
used in the Reznek/Fleishmann *Medea*, 1994–6; Japanese Butoh
which influenced the rehearsal phase of *The Bacchai*, staged at the
Royal National Theatre by Peter Hall in 2002 or the adaptation of
Oedipus at Colonus for a Gospel choir in the USA in 1983. Less
exotically, there are the poetic refigurations in form and imagery such
as the coming together of Latin, Christian and Celtic approaches in
Seamus Heaney's 'Bann Valley Eclogue' (2002) or the use of classical
material as a forum for the meeting of classical and popular art forms
as in Victorian burlesque.[16]

This interaction between classical material and other traditions may
involve a cultural exchange in the meeting of different artistic or
scholarly contexts. It may involve over a period of years or even
centuries various forms of 'migration', across cultures and across
genres. The parameters of cultural history are constantly being
redrawn. Seamus Heaney has put this very clearly when talking
about the history of epic (in this case *Beowulf*):

The study of the history of the English language and of Anglo-Saxon literary texts
means something different now than it did when it was initiated in the 19th century.
Within that older ideological frame, the tracing of Anglo-Saxon origins was as racial
as it was linguistic; there was a definite patriotic purpose to it, a desire to establish the
Anglo-Saxon element as a guarantee of an older, purer English line. . . . But things
are different nowadays. English we now recognise as a confabulation of Englishes
and in current post-colonial conditions, in a devolving Britain, in an evolving Europe,
the more people realise that their language and their culture are historically amassed
possessions, the better. The outlanders at the edge of the world and the speakers at
the bottom of the linguistic pecking order have had their Pentecost . . .These writers
[James Joyce, Hugh MacDiarmid, Derek Walcott, Toni Morrison, Les Murray] and
others like them, sing themselves and celebrate their local idiom as part of the
polyphony that is English. And yet relish of that medium and their enjoyment of their
linguistic independence are all the greater for being based on knowledge of the depth
and distance from which their idiom has sprung. Walcott's sailor hero in his poem

---

[16] See E. Hall, '1845 and all that: singing Greek tragedy on the London stage' in M. Biddiss and
M. Wyke (edd.), *The Uses and Abuses of Antiquity* (Berne, 1999), 37–54, and F. Macintosh, 'Medea
Transposed: Burlesque and Gender on the Mid-Victorian Stage' in E. Hall, F. Macintosh and
O. Taplin (edd.), *Medea in Performance 1500–2000* (Oxford, 2000), 75–99.

'The Schooner Flight', for example, speaks his West Indian English in lines that echo the alliterative metre of Piers Plowman, which in turn is a direct development of the metre of 'Beowulf' . . . Even a slight knowledge of Anglo-Saxon enforces a true, historically based, multi-cultural understanding. And that is to say nothing of the way a feel for the language increases the power of the literature itself.[17]

Heaney associates this kind of cultural shift with a phenomenon that the Russian poet Osip Mandelstam called 'nostalgia for world culture'. This is an ironic use of the word 'nostalgia' to imply something which is not backward-looking but rather aspires to an inter- and cross-cultural creativity that recognizes political and psychological shaping forces. Heaney saw Anglo-Saxon epic as leading to a real historically based cross-cultural understanding. I have quoted the passage almost in full so that the force and structure of his allusions and argument are properly conveyed. It seems to me that at almost every turn one could substitute classical examples and maintain both the coherence of the argument and its power to convince. A model of engagement with classical texts and images as a vehicle for various kinds of cultural exchange and development is perhaps unusual but the direction now being taken by reception studies is revealing precisely that kind of activity. In enabling the seriously inquisitive to distinguish between (for example) the values of a particular appropriating text or society and those of the ancient context of production and to probe the cultural and ideological baggage associated with translational practices, reception studies has had the effect of liberating classical texts and images for a diversity of further refigurations, some of them surprising.

- Processes of cultural and political intervention. The capacity of classical texts to operate in supposedly deserted artistic and political spaces (both ancient and modern) has provided an almost infinitely renewable resource for 'critical distance'. It has enabled social and political critique in censored societies, and in liberal or barely censored contexts has been able to provide a sometimes devastating challenge to conventional wisdoms. Research in progress in the Czech Republic concerning the staging of Greek drama during the period of Soviet domination after the Second World War, suggests that in periods of strong repression translation and staging had to be extremely subtle in order to escape the censor so that it was then left

---

[17] Source: S. Heaney, *Sunday Times* supplement, 26th July 1998.

to the audience to spot hints and make connections. Only as the censorship began to relax could more overt challenges to the regime be staged and some theatrical critics thought that the resulting art forms were cruder and more limited in the ways in which they invited the audience to engage with the plays.[18]

In post-colonial contexts, too, reception of classical texts has been instrumental in the resistance of imposed identities and the construction of new ones. This is true both of post-colonizing societies and of the post-colonized. The common factor in both cases is the potential of classical texts for decolonizing of the mind (of both colonizers and colonized). In this field a look across the different strands in reception studies shows considerable variety in the impact of classical material in pre- and post-independence situations. There have been detailed studies of the impact of the classical aspects of the education system on relationships between ruler and ruled. For example, Jared Majeed has discussed how references to ancient Rome provide an index to British imperialist attitudes to India in the late nineteenth and early twentieth centuries, especially in respect of allusions to the European Classical heritage, Latin and Greek as Indo-European languages, Roman law and the history of the Roman Empire.[19] Tony Harrison's adaptation of Euripides' *Hippolytus* and Seneca's *Phaedra, Phaedra Britannica* (1975) used the setting of the British Raj in India for a critique of race, colonizers and cultural assumptions.[20] Harrison also critiqued Anglo-Egyptian power relations in the archaeological sequences in *The Trackers of Oxyrynchus* adapted from Sophocles' fragmentary *Ichneutai* and staged at Delphi in 1988.[21]

The double-edged impact of classical education as part of colonial education in the British Empire has been demonstrated in the ways in which writers such as Derek Walcott in the Caribbean and Fémi Òsòfisan, Christopher Okigbo, Ola Rotimi and Wole Soyinka in West Africa have used classical themes as a basis for new work which both challenges colonialist and neo-colonialist attitudes and also critiques the politics of their own independent nations. Rotimi's *The Gods Are Not To Blame*, first performed in 1968, explores the themes of Sophocles'

---

[18] A paper on this research was given at an international graduate students' conference in Oxford in summer 2002 by Katerina Kvízová, Institute of Classical Studies, Prague.

[19] J. Majeed, 'Comparativism and references to Rome in British imperial attitudes to India' in C. Edwards (ed.), *Roman Presences: Receptions of Rome in European Culture, 1789–1945* (Cambridge, 1999), 88–109.

[20] Published text in Tony Harrison, *Dramatic Verse 1973–1985* (Newcastle upon Tyne, 1985).

[21] Published text, Tony Harrison, *The Trackers of Oxyrynchus* (London, 1990).

Oedipus the King.[22] It includes lines spoken or sung in Yoruba and is often interpreted as an allegory for the fighting in the Biafran war, while Òsòfisan's *Tegonni: an African Antigone,* first staged in 1994 as part of the Brave New Work project at Emory University, Atlanta, Georgia, USA, refigures Sophocles in a nineteenth-century context to address racial and imperialist problems as well as developing a critique of modern power struggles.[23]

Apart from their intrinsic artistic merit these are significant documents in cultural history. They demonstrate a double consciousness of the historical and artistic role of classical culture – on the one hand appropriated to justify the supposed cultural superiority of colonial role and then re-appropriated to show that the capacity to refigure ancient texts is not confined to the colonizers. The texts raise issues concerning the relationship between individual, social and political responsibilities that can be contextualized in different cultures and historical situations. In this sense, the reception of classical texts by writers in newly independent nations demonstrates that colonization is no longer a constraint on mind and thought but rather that classical material can become one aspect in the creation of new post-colonial senses of identity. When the Kenyan writer and critic Ngũgĩ wa Thiong'o attacked imperialism as a destroyer of culture, an inducer of shame for names, systems of belief, languages, lore, art, dance, song, sculpture, colour he did not intend to comment on the way in which African refigurations of Greek drama and poetry have revived appreciation of precisely those elements of Greek culture, marginalized in some narrower western appropriations but revitalized through encounter with the traditions of African theatre. It is ironic that classically educated African writers were able to do this precisely at a time when classics had been decentred from the curriculum in the colonizing countries. In this sense classical texts may be said to be themselves part of a diaspora, firstly from Greece, then from western Europe and then like other diasporas developing new and hybrid identities in a variety of civic contexts.[24]

Asking questions about the extent to which and how reception practices and scholarship matter and how they make their impact has also to move beyond description and analysis. The lines of enquiry that I

[22] Published text (Oxford, 1971).
[23] Published text in F. Òsòfisan, *Recent Outings* (Ibadan, 1999).
[24] For further discussion see L. Hardwick, 'Greek Drama and Anti–colonialism: Decolonising Classics' in E. Hall, F. Macintosh and A. Wrigley (edd.), *Dionysus Since '69* (Oxford, 2003).

have sketched out above suggest to me that new kinds of evaluation are also emerging. In these, 'faithfulness' to a unified interpretation of an ancient text is no longer a defining criterion. Instead, investigating the *nature* of the relationship between ancient and modern, and between these and other mediating texts and contexts, may generate other kinds of evaluative terms: 'questioning', 'challenging', 'unexpected', 'celebratory', 'selective', 'subversive' may partner 'profound' and 'revealing'. In the reception vocabulary of the future, appreciation of formal technique may be matched by appreciation of cultural hybridity and energy and an awareness of cultural fragmentation and regrouping. Above all, reception studies have shown that classical texts, images and ideas are culturally active presences. The vocabulary of reception studies has moved on from notions of 'legacy' to include also the values and practices of the present and future creativity of classical culture. The key evaluative question both for the relationship with the past and for the present, may well be 'what difference was made?' This question covers both the practices of the appropriator or agent of refiguration in relation to the source text or idea and additionally the impact on the receiving culture or tradition. There are three aspects which are the main aids to judgement on these questions. Firstly, have the artists 'made' or created a work which differs in significant respects from the classical text or image? If so, how is this difference expressed? Formally? Linguistically? Visually? And how do such differences correspond to the differences and similarities between the ancient and subsequent contexts of production and reception? Are we dealing with what might be termed an imitation, an analogue or a totally new work?

Secondly, how does the imitation, analogue or new work affect perceptions of the ancient world? Does it prompt the receiving individuals or groups to revisit the ancient works, perhaps to find elements which had been concealed or marginalized; does it reject aspects of the ancient; does it explicitly or implicitly appropriate aspects of the ancient as artistic, cultural or political examples or foundation myths to give authority to contemporary practices or ideas? Does it recuperate or regenerate ancient practices in a way which makes them more acceptable or comprehensible to a subsequent society? Does it regrow these in different cultural ground?

And thirdly, what do the modern work and its reception suggest about the direction of contemporary aesthetic and cultural practices? Does it stimulate debate, offer insights and critique and transform perspectives; does it appeal to an unchanging aesthetic standard or notion of human nature; does it reaffirm certain kinds of values in a different context?

Some of these judgements about the making of differences and their impact require time and critical distance before they can be made. In this respect the study of very recent appropriations and refigurations has special requirements for the finding, preservation and analysis of the data which will inform judgements that can only be made in the future. The growth of reception studies in recent years contains an explicit claim that classical culture will continue to be a significant strand in cultural history. It also implies a requirement to develop transparent rationales and practices in cultural philology that will make critical enquiry a reality in the present and form a coherent basis for investigation by the cultural historians of the future.

BIBLIOGRAPHY

Ades, D., Benton, T., Elliott, D. and Whyte, I.B. (1995): *Art and Power: Europe under the Dictators 1930–1945* Hayward Gallery Exhibition Catalogue (Manchester).

Baker, M., ed. (1997): *The Routledge Encyclopaedia of Translation Studies* (London and New York).

Balme, Christopher B. (1997): 'Interpreting the Pictorial Record: Theatre Iconography and the Referential Dilemma' in *Theatre Research International* (Special Edition, Theatre and Iconography) vol. 22 no. 3, 180–201.

Barlow, S., ed. (1986): tr. and commentary Euripides, *Trojan Women* (Warminister).

Beacham, R.C. (1995): *The Roman Theatre and its Audience* (London).

Beevor, A. (1998 and 1999): *Stalingrad* (London).

—— (2002): *Berlin: the Downfall, 1945* (London).

Bennett, S. (1990): *Theatre Audiences: a Theory of Production and Reception* (London and New York).

Benton, T. (1995): 'Rome reclaims its Empire: Architecture' and 'Speaking without Adjectives: Architecture in the Service of Totalitarianism' in D. Ades *et al.* (edd.) (1995), 120–28.

Biddis, M., Wyke, M., edd. (1999): *The Uses and Abuses of Antiquity* (Berne).

Bolgar, R. R. (1954): *The Classical Heritage and its Beneficiaries* (Cambridge).

—— (1981): 'The Greek Legacy' in Finley, M. I. (1981), 429–72.

Bowker, L., Cronin, M., Kenny, D., and Pearson, J. (1998): *Unity in Diversity? Current Trends in Translation Studies* (Manchester).

Brathwaite, K. (1967): *Odale's Choice* (London, reprinted 1993).

Braund, Susanna Morton (2002): *Latin Literature* (London and New York).

Brown, I., Ramage, J. and Sherlock, C. (2000): 'Scots and Welsh: Theatrical Translation and Theatrical Languages', *International Journal of Scottish Theatre* vol. 1 no. 2 at http://arts.qmuc.ac.uk/ijost/Volume1_no2/I_Brown.htm.

Brown, J. R., ed. (1995): *The Oxford Illustrated History of Theatre* (Oxford).

Brown, Peter G. McC. (2002): 'Actors and actor-managers at Rome at the time of Plautus and Terence' in Easterling P. and Hall E., *Greek and Roman Actors: Aspects of an Ancient Profession* (Cambridge), 225–37.

Budelmann, F. and Michelakis, P., edd. (2001): *Homer, Tragedy and Beyond: Essays in honour of P. E. Easterling* (London).

Burke, A. (2001): 'Totalitarianism, Martyrdom and Social Resistance: Sarah Wood's *Antigone*', *International Journal of Scottish Theatre* vol. 2 no. 1, September 2001, 26pp. http://arts.qmuc.ac.uk/ijost/Volume1_no3.

—— (2003): A critical study of the role of the theatre practitioner interview in reception research is being conducted by Alison Burke and will be published in 2003 at http://www2.open.ac.uk/ClassicalStudies/GreekPlays/Webpages/essays/essaypage.htm.

Burkert, W. (1992): *The Orientalising Revolution: Near Eastern Influence on Greek Culture – the early Archaic Age* (Cambridge, Mass. and London).

Burian, P. (1997): 'Tragedy adapted for stages and screens: the Renaissance to the present' in Easterling, ed. (1997), 228–83.

Burrow, C. (1997): 'Virgils from Dante to Milton' in Martindale C. ed., *The Cambridge Companion to Virgil* (Cambridge), 79–90.

Canitz, A.E. Christa (1996): 'In our Awyn Language: the National Agenda of Gavin Douglas "Eneados"', *Virgilius*, 25–37.

Cartledge, Paul (2002): 'Greek civilisation and slavery' in Wiseman T.P. ed. (2002), 247–62.

Chamberlain, Julie (2002): *Coventry Evening Telegraph*, 1st June 2002, p. 11.

Chioles, J. (1993): '*The Oresteia* and the *avant-garde*: three decades of discourse', *Performing Arts Journal*, no. 45, 1–28.

Christie, I. (2000): 'Between Magic and Realism: Medea on Film', in Hall E., Macintosh F. and Taplin O., *Medea in Performance* (Oxford), 144–65.

Clarke, G.W., ed. (1989): *Rediscovering Hellenism: the Hellenic Inheritance and the English Imagination* (Cambridge).

Csapo, E. and Slater W.J. (1995): *The Context of Ancient Drama* (Michigan).

Davies, J.K. (2002): 'Greek History: a Discipline in Transformation' in Wiseman, T.P. ed. (2002), 225–46.

Denard, H. (2000): 'Seamus Heaney, Colonialism and the Cure', *PAJ: A Journal of Performance and Art* 22.3, 1–18.

Donaldson, Ian (1982): *The Rape of Lucretia: a Myth and its Transformation* (Oxford).

Douglas, K. (1988): *The Ragman's Son: an Autobiography* (New York).

Dryden, J. (1680): Preface to translation of *Ovid's Epistles*.

du Bois, Page (2001): *Trojan Horses: Saving the Classics from Conservatives* (New York and London).

Duffy, Carol Ann (1999): *The World's Wife* (Basingstoke and Oxford).

Dunlop, Bill (1993): *Klytemnestra's Bairns* (Edinburgh).

——(2000): 'Klytemnestra's Bairns: Adapting Aeschylus into Scots', *International Journal of Scottish Theatre*, vol. 1 no. 1, http://arts.qmuc.ac.uk/ijost/Volume1_no1/BDunlop.htm.

Easterling, P. (1981): 'Greek Plays at Cambridge' in *Le Théâtre Antique de Nos Jours: Symposium International à Delphes 18–21 Août 1981* (Athens), 89–94.

——(1985): 'Greek Literature', in Easterling, P.E. and Knox, B.M.W. edd. *The Cambridge History of Classical Literature* vol. 1 ch. 1 (Cambridge).

——ed. (1997): *The Cambridge Companion to Greek Tragedy* (Cambridge).

——(1999): 'The early years of the Cambridge Greek Play' in C.A. Stray ed.

Classics in Nineteenth and Twentieth Century Cambridge: Curriculum, Culture and Community, Cambridge *PCPS Supplement* 24, 27–47.

—— (2002): 'A taste for the Classics' in Wiseman, ed. (2002), 21–37.

Easterling, P. and Hall, E. edd. (2002): *Greek and Roman Actors: Aspects of an Ancient Profession* (Cambridge).

Edwards. C. ed. (1999): *Roman Presences: Receptions of Rome in European Culture, 1789–1945* (Cambridge and New York).

Emlyn-Jones, C., Hardwick, L. and Purkis, J. edd. (1992): *Homer: Readings and Images* (London).

Ewans, M. (1982): *Wagner and Aeschylus: the Ring and the Oresteia* (London).

Fast, H. (1951): *Spartacus* (New York), with further editions 1958, 1960, 1997.

Finley, M.I., ed. (1981): *The Legacy of Greece* (Oxford).

Fischer-Lichte, Erika (1992): *The Semiotics of Theatre*, tr. Jeremy Gaines and Doris L. Jones (Bloomington and Indianapolis) (originally published in three volumes in 1983 as *Semiotik des Theaters*, Tübingen).

Fitzpatrick, D., Hardwick, L., Ireland, S., and Montserrat, D. edd. (2002): *Old Wine, New Bottles: Texts for Classics in a Changed Learning Environment at University* (Milton Keynes).

Gadamer, H-G. (1975): *Truth and Method* (New York) first published 1960, the tr. G. Barden and J. Cumming (1975) used the second edition, 1965.

Gamel, Mary-Kay (1991): 'American Tragedy: *Chinatown*' in Martin M. Winkler ed., *Classics and Cinema*, Bucknell Review, 209–31.

Golder, H. (1996): 'Geek Tragedy? Why I'd rather go to the movies', *Arion*, third series 4.1 (Spring).

Goldhill, S., ed. (2001): *Being Greek Under Rome* (Cambridge).

—— (2002): *Who Needs Greek? Contests in the Cultural History of Hellenism* (Cambridge).

Goldhill, S. and Osborne, R. edd. (1999): *Performance Culture and Athenian Democracy* (Cambridge).

Gombrich, Ernst (1960): *Art and Illusion* (Princeton).

Grant, Barry Keith (1986): *Film Genre Reader* (Austin).

Green, J.R. (2000): 'Forty Years of Theatre Research and its future directions' in Hardwick, L., Easterling, P.E., Ireland, S., Lowe, N. and Macintosh, F. edd. *Theatre: Ancient and Modern* (Milton Keynes), 1–20, and is also available electronically at http://www.open.ac.uk/Arts/CC99/green.html.

Hall, E. (1999): '1845 and all that: singing Greek tragedy on the London stage' in Biddiss, M. and Wyke, M. edd., 37–54.

—— (2002): 'Tony Harrison's *Prometheus*: a View from the Left', *Arion*, Spring/Summer, Third Series, vol. 10, no. 1.

Hall, E., Macintosh, F., and Taplin, O. edd. (2000): *Medea in Performance, 1500–2000* (Oxford).

Hall, E. Macintosh, F., and Wrigley, A. edd. (2003): *Dionysus since '69* (Oxford, forthcoming).

Halliwell, S. (1989): 'Aristotle's *Poetics*' in Kennedy, G.A., ed., 149–83.

Hardie, P. (1998): *Virgil*, New Surveys in the Classics, no. 28 (Oxford).

Hardwick, L. (1992): 'Convergence and Divergence in Reading Homer' in Emlyn-Jones, C. et al., edd., 227–48.

—— (1995): 'Classical distances' in Sewart, D. ed., 283–6.

—— (1997): 'Reception as Simile: the Poetics of Reversal in Homer and Derek Walcott', *International Journal of the Classical Tradition* vol. 3, Winter, 326–38.

—— (2000): *Translating Words, Translating Cultures* (London).

—— (2000): *Tony Harrison's Poetry, Drama and Film: the Classical Dimension*, The Open Colloquium 1999 (Milton Keynes), 16–28 and electronically at http://www.open.ac.uk/Arts/Colq99/MacFinal.htm.

—— (2001): 'The Theatrical Review as a Primary Source for the Modern Reception of Greek Drama: a preliminary evaluation', http://www2.open.a-c.uk/ClassicalStudies/GreekPlays/Webpages/Projectsite/Reviews.html.

—— (2001): 'Who owns the plays? Issues in Translation and Performance of Greek Drama on the Modern Stage', *Eirene* XXXVII, Special Edition Theatralia, 23–39.

—— (2002): '*Electra* and The Theatre of Affliction: towards a textual turn?', *Didaskalia*, special edition on Sophocles' *Electra*, published electronically at www.didaskalia.net.

—— (2003): 'Contemporary Receptions of Homer' in Fowler, R., ed., *The Cambridge Handbook to Homer* (Cambridge, forthcoming).

—— (2003): 'Classical Theatre in Modern Scotland – a democratic stage?' in Hardwick, L. and Gillespie, C., edd., *Crossing Boundaries through Greek Tragedy*, Selected Proceedings of the Open Colloquium (Milton Keynes).

—— (2003): 'Greek Drama and anti-colonialism: Decolonising Classics' in Hall, E., Macintosh, F., and Wrigley, A., edd., *Dionysus Since '69* (Oxford, forthcoming).

—— (2003/4): 'Staging Agamemnon: the Languages of Translation' in Macintosh, F. ed., *Agamemnon Staged: Proceedings of the* Agamemnon *Conference 2001* (Oxford).

—— (forthcoming): 'Seamus Heaney's Classical Ground'.

—— (ongoing): *Reception of Greek Texts and Images in Late 20th Century Drama and Poetry in English* Database http://www2.open.ac.uk/ClassicalStudies/GreekPlays/.

Harrison, S.J. (1990): *Oxford Readings in Vergil's Aeneid* (Oxford).

—— (1990) 'Some views of the *Aeneid* in the Twentieth Century' in Harrison, S.J. ed., 1–20.

Harrison, S.J. (2001): *Texts, Ideas and the Classics* (Oxford).

Harrison, T. (1985): *Dramatic Verse 1973–1985* (Newcastle upon Tyne).

—— (1990): *The Trackers of Oxyrynchus* (London).

—— (1992): *The Gaze of the Gorgon* (Newcastle upon Tyne).

—— (1996): *Plays 3* (London).

—— (1998): *Prometheus* (Newcastle upon Tyne).

Hartigan, K. (1995): *Greek Tragedy on the American Stage: Ancient Drama in the Commercial Theater, 1882–1994* (Westport, CT and London).

Heaney, S. (1990): *The Cure at Troy* (London).

—— (2001): *Electric Light* (London).

Highet, G. (1949): *The Classical Tradition: Greek and Roman Influences on Western Literature* (Oxford).

Hitler, A. (1953): *Table Talk*, tr. N. Cameron and R.C.H. Stevens (London).

Hobsbawm, E. (1995): Forward to Ades, D. *et al.*, edd.

Holub, Robert C. (1984): *Reception Theory: a Critical Introduction* (London).

Iser, W. (1978): *The Act of Reading: a Theory of Aesthetic Response* (Baltimore and London).

Jauss, H.R. (1982): *Towards an Aesthetic of Reception*, tr. T. Bahti (Minneapolis).

Jenkyns, R. (1980): *The Victorians and Ancient Greece* (Oxford).

—— (1992): *The Legacy of Rome, a New Appraisal* (Oxford).

Jorgens, Jack J. (1977): *Shakespeare on Film* (Bloomington).

Kennedy, G.A. (1989): *The Cambridge History of Classical Literary Criticism*, vol. 1 (Cambridge).

Koestler, A. (1939): *The Gladiators*, tr. Edith Simon (London), 2nd edition, New York, 1956, 1962 and with new postscript, New York, 1965.

Laurence, Ray (1999): 'Tourism, town planning and *romanitas*: Rimini's Roman heritage', in Wyke and Biddiss (edd.), *The Uses and Abuses of Antiquity* (Bern, Berlin, Bruxelles, Frankfurt and New York).

Leatherman, LeRoy (1966): *Martha Graham: Portrait of the Lady as an Artist* (New York).

Lichtheim, M. (1976): *Ancient Egyptian Literature* vol. 2: *the New Kingdom* (Berkeley, Los Angeles, London).

Llewellyn-Jones, L. (2003): 'Trasidei Gymraeg: Is there a Classical Tradition in Welsh Language Drama?' in Hardwick and Gillespie edd.

Lloyd-Jones, H. (1982): *Aeschylus: Oresteia* (London).

—— (1998): 'Interesting Times', *International Journal of the Classical Tradition*, vol. 4 no. 4, Spring, 580–613.

Logue, C. (1999): *Homer: War Music* (London).

Longley, M. (1991): *Gorse Fires* (London).

—— (1995): *The Ghost Orchid* (London).

Losemann, Volker (1999): 'The Nazi Concept of Rome' in Edwards ed., 221–35.

Lowell, Robert, tr. (1978): *Oresteia of Aeschylus* (New York).

Macintosh, F. (1995): 'Under the Blue Pencil: Greek Tragedy and the British Censor', *Dialogos* 2, 54–70.

—— (1997): 'Tragedy in Performance: nineteenth- and twentieth-century productions' in Easterling ed., *The Cambridge Companion to Greek Tragedy* (Cambridge), 284–323.

—— (2000): 'Medea Transposed: Burlesque and Gender on the Mid-Victorian Stage' in Hall, Macintosh and Taplin edd., *Medea in Performance 1500–2000* (Oxford), 75–99.

—— (2003/4): *Agamemnon Staged: Proceedings of the* Agamemnon *Conference 2001* (Oxford).

MacKinnon, K. (1986): *Greek Tragedy into Film* (London).

—— (2000): 'Film Adaptation on the Myth of Textual Fidelity' in Hardwick, ed. (Milton Keynes), 16–28 and electronically at http://www.open.ac.uk/Arts/Colq99/MacFinal.htm.

Majeed, J. (1999): 'Comparativism and references to Rome in British imperial attitudes to India' in Edwards, ed., *Roman Presences: Receptions of Rome in European Culture, 1789–1945* (Cambridge), 88–109.

Mandela, N. (1994 and 1995): *Long Walk to Freedom* (London).

March, J. (1987): *The Creative Poet*, ICS Bulletin Supplement 49 (London), 79–118.

Martindale, C. (1993): *Redeeming the Text: Latin Poetry and the Hermeneutics of Reception* (Cambridge).

—— ed. (1997): *The Cambridge Companion to Virgil* (Cambridge).

Massinger, P. (2002): *The Roman Actor* (London).

McDonald, M. (2000): '*Medea è mobile*: the Many Faces of Medea in Opera' in Hall, Macintosh and Taplin edd., *Medea in Performance, 1500–2000* (Oxford), 100–18.

Meech, A. (2000): 'The Irrepressible in Pursuit of the Impossible, Translating the Theatre of the GDR' in Carole-Anne Upton, ed., *Moving Target: Theatre Translation and Cultural Relocation* (Manchester), 127–37.

Meineck, P. (1998): *Aristophanes* (*Clouds, Wasps, Birds*) (Indianapolis and Cambridge).

Mezzabotta, M. (2000): 'Ancient Greek Drama in the New South Africa', in Hardwick *et al.* edd., 246–68, and also at http://www.open.ac.uk/Arts/CC99/mezza.htm.

Michelakis, P. (2001): 'The past as a foreign country? Greek tragedy, cinema and the politics of space' in Budelmann, F. and Michelakis, P. edd., *Homer, Tragedy and Beyond: Essays in honour of P. E. Easterling* (London), 241–57, including filmography.

Morris, S.P. (1992): *Daidalos and the Origins of Greek Arts* (Princeton).

Murray, P. (2000): *Classical Literary Criticism*, tr. P. Murray and T.S. Dorsch (London).

Òsòfisan, F. (1999): *Recent Outings* (Ibadan).

Parker, J. (2000): *Dialogic Education and the Problematics of Translation in Homer and Greek Tragedy* (Lampeter, Ontario and New York).

Patsalidis, S. and Sakellaridou, E, edd. (1999): *(Dis)placing Classical Greek Theatre* (Thessaloniki).

Reading, P. (1996): *Collected Poems* 2 (Newcastle upon Tyne).

Reynolds, L.D. and Wilson, N.G. (1974): *Scribes and Scholars: a Guide to the Transmission of Greek and Latin Literature* (Oxford, 2nd edition).

Robinson, P. (2000): 'Facing up to the Unbearable: the Mythical Method in Tony Harrison's Film/Poems' in Hardwick, ed., *Tony Harrison's Poetry, Drama and Film: the Classical Dimension*, Proceedings of the Open Colloquium 1999 (Milton Keynes), 29–43 and electronically at http://www.open.ac.uk/Arts/Colq99/robinson.htm.

Rosenberg, I. (1979): *The Collected Works of Isaac Rosenberg: Poetry, Prose, Letters, Paintings and Drawings*, ed. I. Parsons (London).

Roueché, C. (1993): *Performers and Partisans at Aphrodisias in the Roman and Late Roman Periods*, *JRS* Monograph 6 (London).

Rouse, R.H. (1992): 'The Transmission of the Texts' in Jenkyns, ed., 37–59.

Russell, D.A. and Winterbottom, M, edd. (1989): *Classical Literary Criticism* (Oxford).

Schmidt, Peter Lebrecht (2001): 'Latin Studies in Germany 1933–1945: Institutional Conditions, Political Pressures, Scholarly Consequences' in Harrison, ed., 285–300.

Schofield, M. (2002): 'Socrates on Trial in the USA' in Wiseman, ed.

Seldes, G. (1935): *Sawdust Caesar: the Untold History of Mussolini and Fascism* (New York and London).

Sewart, D. (1995): *One World Many Voices* vol. 1 (Milton Keynes).

Shaw, Brent D. (2001): *Spartacus and the Slave Wars: a Brief History with Documents* (Boston and New York).

Sherlock, C. (1998): '*Antigone*, a Scots/Welsh Experience of Mythical and Theatrical Translation' in Bowker L., Cronin M., Kenny D. and Pearson J. edd. (1998), 25–37.

Silk, M. (2000): *Aristophanes and the Definition of Comedy* (Oxford).

Sobchack, Thomas (1975): 'Genre Film: A Classical Experience', first published in *Literature/Film Quarterly* 3, 196–204 and reprinted in Barry Keith Grant, ed., *Film Genre Reader* (Austin, 1986); quoted and discussed by Mary-Kay Gamel, 'American Tragedy: *Chinatown*' in Martin M. Winkler, ed., *Classics and Cinema*, Bucknell Review, 1991, 209–31.

Sommerstein, Alan, tr. (1973): *Aristophanes, Lysistrata* (London).

Stanford, W.B. (1976): *Ireland and the Classical Tradition* (Dublin).

Stone, Marla (1999): 'A flexible Rome: Fascism and the cult of *romanità*' in Edwards ed., 188–220.

Stray, C. A. (1998): *Classics Transformed: Schools, Universities and Society in England, 1830–1960* (Oxford).

—— ed. (2000): *Classics in Nineteenth and Twentieth Century Cambridge: Curriculum, Culture and Community*, *PCPS* Supplement 24 (Cambridge).

Stuttard, D., tr. (1999): *Agamemnon* (York).

——tr. (2000): *Trojan Women* (York).

Swan, S. (1996): *Hellenism and Empire: Language, Classicism and Power in the Greek World AD50–250* (Oxford).

Taplin, O. (1977): *The Stagecraft of Aeschylus* (Oxford).

——(1978): *Greek Tragedy in Action* (London).

——(1993): *Comic Angels and Other Approaches to Greek Drama through Vase-Paintings* (Oxford).

——(2002): 'Contemporary Poetry and Classics' in Wiseman, ed.

Tudeau-Clayton, M. (1999): 'Richard Carew, William Shakespeare, and the Politics of Translating Virgil in Early Modern England and Scotland', *International Journal of the Classical Tradition*, vol. 5 no. 4 (Spring), 507–27.

Turner, F.M. (1981): *The Greek Heritage in Victorian Britain* (Yale).

Turner, G. (1993): *Film as Social Practice* (London).

Underwood, Simeon (1998): *English Translators of Homer from George Chapman to Christopher Logue* (London).

Upton, Carole-Anne (2000): *Moving Target: Theatre Translation and Cultural Relocation* (Manchester).

Vellacott, Philip, tr. (1959): *The Oresteian Trilogy* (Harmondsworth).

Walcott, D. (1990): *Omeros* (London).

——(1993): *The Odyssey: a Stage Version* (London).

Walder, D. (1992): 'Resituating Fugard: South African Drama as Witness', *New Theatre Quarterly* 8/32 (November), 343–61.

Weber, W. (1936): *Princeps: Studien zur Geschichte des Augustes* (Stuttgart).

West, M.L. (1997): *The East Face of Helicon: West Asiatic Elements in Greek Poetry and Myth* (Oxford).

Whitmarsh, T. (2001): *Greek Literature and the Roman Empire* (Cambridge).

Wiles, D. (1995): 'Theatre in Roman and Christian Europe' in Brown, J.R., ed., *The Oxford Illustrated History of Theatre* (Oxford), 49-92.

——(1997): *Tragedy in Athens: Performance Space and Theatrical Meaning* (Cambridge).

——(2000): *Greek Theatre Performance: an Introduction* (Cambridge).

——(2003): 'The use of masks in modern performances of Greek drama' in Hall, Macintosh and Wrigley, edd., *Dionysus since '69* (Oxford, forthcoming).

Wilmer, S.E. (1999): 'Seamus Heaney and the tragedy of stasis' in Patsalidis and Sakellaridou, edd., *(Dis)placing Classical Greek Theatre* (Thessaloniki), 221-31.

Winkler, Martin M., ed. (1991): *Classics and Cinema*, Bucknell Review.

Wiseman, T.P. ed. (2002): *Classics in Progress: Essays on Ancient Greece and Rome* (Oxford).

Woolf, G.D. (1994): 'Becoming Roman, staying Greek: culture, identity and the civilizing process in the Roman East', *Proceedings of the Cambridge Philological Society* 40.

Wrigley, Amanda (2002): 'Review of Royal National Theatre's *Bacchai*', *JACT Review*, second series, no. 32 (autumn), 12–14.

Wyke, Maria (1997): *Projecting the Past: Ancient Rome, Cinema and History* (New York and London).

—— (1999): 'Screening Ancient Rome in the New Italy' in Edwards, ed., *Roman Presences: Receptions of Rome in European Culture, 1789–1945* (Cambridge).

—— (1999): 'Sawdust Caesar: Mussolini, Julius Caesar and the drama of dictatorship' in Wyke and Biddiss, edd., *The Uses and Abuses of Antiquity* (Bern, Berlin, Bruxelles, Frankfurt and New York).

Ziolkowski, Theodore (2000): 'The Fragmented Text: The Classics and Postwar European Literature', *International Journal of the Classical Tradition*, vol. 6 no. 4 (spring), 549–62.

SUPPLEMENTARY BIBLIOGRAPHY

Reception studies make use of dual perspectives which analyse not only the source text and the shifts of emphasis in its receptions but also the situation of the reception within the non-classical traditions which have helped to generate it. Thus the demands for interdisciplinary analysis are potentially very great. In the body of this Survey, bibliographical references were confined to works which directly addressed the texts and issues under discussion. The material which follows outlines some possibilities for wider reading and suggests material which will augment the first essential – the texts of the sources and receptions themselves.

REFERENCE WORKS

The Oxford Classical Dictionary (edd. S. Hornblower and A. Spawforth, 3rd edition (Oxford, 1996)) has significant entries on reception, translation and literary theory and classical studies (although not on transmission, which has to be approached via the entries on libraries and books). There is useful material in *The Encyclopaedia of Greece and the Hellenic Tradition* (ed. G. Speake, 2 vols (London, 2000)), in Eric Smith, ed., *A Dictionary of Classical Reference in English Poetry* (Cambridge, 1984), in the forthcoming *New Dictionary of National Biography* (ed. B. Harrison (Oxford, 2003–)), in the forthcoming *Dictionary of British Classicists* (ed. R. Todd (Bristol, 2004)) and in W. Briggs, ed., *The Biographical Dictionary of North American Classicists* (1994).

JOURNALS

An increasing number of classical and literary journals publish articles on various aspects of classical reception studies. The most useful include *The International Journal of the Classical Tradition* (which publishes in English, German and French), *Akroterion* (essential for study of reception in South Africa), *Arethusa, Arion, Classical and Modern Literature, Didaskalia* (an electronic journal covering reception of Greek and Roman drama), *Eirene* (which draws on research in central and eastern Europe as well as the west), *Scholia, Translation and Literature* (wide-ranging and frequently includes articles and reviews on classical texts and their translation and reception). Also relevant are a number of theatre research journals such as *PAJ: A Journal of the Performing Arts, Theatre Journal* and *Theatre Research International*. For an annotated list of journals which publish research on the reception of Greek drama, consult Ruth Hazel, *Bibliography of Theatre Journals, Periodicals and other Resources* (Milton Keynes, 2001) (also available electronically at http://www2.open.ac.uk/ClassicalStudies/GreekPlays).

TRANSLATION

There are chapters on theoretical and generic approaches and on translations of Greek and Latin authors in P. France, ed., *The Oxford Guide to Literature in English Translation* (Oxford, 2000). This indispensable volume includes detailed bibliographies on each topic discussed, together with a more general list of further reading. Particularly useful Readers are D. Robinson, ed., *Western Translation Theory from Herodotus to Nietzsche* (Manchester, 1997), which includes lengthy excerpts from ancient authors, and L. Venuti, ed., *The Translation Studies Reader* (London and New York, 2000), which focuses on modern approaches. Forthcoming publications which will include substantial treatments of classical material are A.P. Frank *et al.*, edd., *Übersetzung, Translation, Traduction, An International Encyclopaedia of Translation Studies* (Berlin/New York), many vols, and P. France and S. Gillespie, edd., *The Oxford History of Literary Translation in English*, 5 vols. For broader interpretations of literary translations and adaptations, see G. Steiner, *After Babel: Aspects of Language and Translation* (Oxford, 1975, 2nd edition 1992), and L. Hardwick, *Translating Words, Translating Cultures* (London, 2000), which considers works which move classical texts and referents across boundaries of culture and literary tradition.

LANGUAGE AND RECEPTION

There is an essay on the influence of the Latin language by Rebecca Posner, 'Language' in R. Jenkyns, ed., *The Legacy of Rome: a New Appraisal* (Oxford, 1992). However, in order to study the impact of Greek and Roman works on other languages via translation and the impact of the translations on understanding of the Greek and Roman sources, it is necessary to range more widely. The problems and opportunities in reading classical texts in translations in which some words are left in the original are discussed in J. Parker, *Dialogic Education and the Problematics of Translation in Homer and Greek Tragedy* (Lewiston, Queenstown, Lampeter, 2001). J. Derrick McLure, *Language, Poetry and Nationhood – Scots as a Poetic Language from 1878 to the Present* (East Linton, 2000), offers some important methodological pointers and suggests issues for debate, with passing attention to some classical referents. A. Bery and P. Murray, edd., *Comparing Postcolonial Literatures* (New York and Basingstoke, 2000), contains provocative studies of diaspora, hybridity and African modernism which impinge on, although they do not directly discuss, classical receptions. Ismail S. Talib, *The Language of Postcolonial Literatures*

(London and New York, 2002) discusses how the English language has contended with and been shaped by other languages in postcolonial contexts and the book therefore informs study of important areas of classical reception.

ANTHOLOGIES, COMPANIONS AND SURVEYS

Comparative use of anthologies is a good way of tracking changes in the popularity of and the significance attributed to classical material, especially poetry. Anthologies of classical poetry, arranged chronologically or by 'period', 'movement' or individual author provide useful interfaces and allow study of patterns of excerpting as well as of selection of individual authors and poems. A good starting point is A. Poole and J. Maule, edd., *The Oxford Book of Classical Verse in Translation* (Oxford, 1995). For study of individual authors, the Penguin Classics series includes volumes on *Homer in English* (ed. G. Steiner, 1996), *Virgil in English* (ed. K.W. Gransden, 1996), *Horace in English* (ed. D.S. Carne-Ross and K. Haynes, 1996), *Ovid in English* (ed. C. Martin, 1998), *Martial in English* (ed. J.P. Sullivan and A.J. Boyle, 1996) and *Seneca in English* (ed. D. Share, 1998). Also important for study of classical receptions is *Dante in English* (ed. E. Griffiths and M. Reynolds, 1999). Larger contextual studies are facilitated by S. Deane, ed., *The Field Day Anthology of Irish Writing* (Derry 1991), 3 vols, which includes an introductory essay and a significant number of classical adaptations from Early and Middle Irish literature to the present day.

The *Cambridge Companion* series includes volumes on *Greek Tragedy* (ed. P. Easterling, 1997); *Virgil* (ed. C. Martindale, 1997); *Ovid* (ed. P. Hardie, 2002) and *Homer* (ed. R. Fowler, 2003 forthcoming). There are interesting differences in selection and arrangement of the treatment of reception in each of these volumes. The Greek Tragedy and Ovid Companions each include substantial chapters on reception (six for Ovid, four for Tragedy) and these are placed in a separate section at the end. The Virgil volume starts with a section of seven chapters on 'Translation and Reception' and puts study of content and form in a section at the end of the book. The Homer Companion will include discussion of the problems involved in making judgements about very recent receptions. Reception issues are increasingly included as a strand in survey studies of individual poets or of classical culture – see the important but tantalizingly brief discussion of 'classic' status and broader aspects of reception in P. Hardie, *Virgil*, New Surveys in the Classics no. 28 (Oxford, 1998), 3–4 and the chapter on reception in B. Sparkes and T.W. Harrison, edd. *The Edinburgh Companion to Ancient Greece and Rome* (Edinburgh, 2004), forthcoming.

THE CLASSICAL TRADITION

The brief discussion of the classical tradition in chapter 1 of this Survey focused on the distinction between the concerns of the classical tradition with largely chronological and mono-cultural 'influences' and the broader inter-textual and interdisciplinary emphases of reception studies. However, the specific concerns of research on the history of the classical tradition and in particular the shifts in its approaches and paradigms are also rewarding areas for further reading. The Preface to R. Jenkyns, ed., *The Legacy of Rome: a New Appraisal* (Oxford, 1992), recognizes these changes and distinguishes between the approach adopted in 1921 by Sir Richard Livingstone in *The Legacy of Greece* (and its companion volume *The Legacy of Rome*, ed. Cyril Bailey, 1923) and those thought appropriate in 1981 in M.I. Finley, ed., *The Legacy of Greece: a New Appraisal*, and its companion, Jenkyns's own volume. Jenkyns's emphasis was on 'the range and diversity of the Roman inheritance' rather than on a general survey of Roman history or culture and he included as contributors alongside classicists those whose expertise was primarily in the history or literature of later times. This indicates a move towards exchange of ideas derived from different approaches (in terms both of theory and of discipline).

The trend identified by Jenkyns was already evident in collections such as the book edited by G.W. Clarke, *Rediscovering Hellenism: the Hellenic Inheritance and the English Imagination* (Cambridge, 1989), which included essays ad-dressing issues of authenticity, Hebraic and Hellenic cultural approaches and the appropriation of Hellenism by the Victorian ruling class. However, not until the collected essays prepared for a British Academy project and edited by T.P. Wiseman, *Classics in Progress: Essays on Ancient Greece and Rome* (Oxford, 2002), did the spotlight turn on a more self-reflexive examination of the diversity and changes in the subject matter and working methods of classical scholarship, including the classical tradition.

Some of these trends, although by no means all, had been anticipated by Gilbert Highet in his famous work *The Classical Tradition: Greek and Roman Influences on Western Literature* (Oxford, 1949). He included chapters on a variety of contemporary approaches and criticized classicists for narrowing the scope of classical work by excluding popular culture and its interfaces with classical texts. Highet's work has been criticized for its emphasis on the unity of Greek and Roman culture and for its dismissive attitude to the loss of 'civilisation' in the Dark Ages but he did provide an overarching chronological framework and explore the significance of successive phases and paradigms in classical influence. He also recognized the importance of interaction with other aspects of the receiving contexts and considered the role of classical scholarship in the transmission, criticism and interpretation of classical texts. He was a vigorous critic of what he regarded as deficiencies in translations by professional scholars and castigated bad teaching. Highet also had a touching, if misplaced, faith in the capacity of classical culture to save the world from 'the repeated attacks of materialism and barbarism' (ch. 21, 500). Quite apart from arguments about the validity of his selections and judgements, Highet's work is an important document in the history of classical scholarship and needs to be revisited as a comparison with the very different approaches to cultural history which are now to be seen in work influenced by anthropological approaches (for example in the work of J-P. Vernant and P. Vidal-Naquet, *Myth and Tragedy in Ancient Greece*, tr. J. Lloyd (New York, 1988, French originals 1972 and 1986) or by cultural theory (for example, T. Eagleton, *Sweet Violence: the Idea of the Tragic* (Oxford, 2002)).

Other strands in works situated within the framework of the classical tradition are those directly concerned with the history and sociology of scholarship. Of these, the most significant in recent years include Hellmut Flashar, ed., *Altertums Wissenschaft in dem 20er Jahren: Neue Fragen und Impulse* (Stuttgart, 1995) and C.A. Stray, *Classics Transformed: Schools, Universities and Society in England 1830–1960* (Oxford, 1998). Unfortunately, most of the essays in Flashar's volume have not yet been translated from the German. However, there is a detailed Review Essay, with extensive further bibliography by H. Lloyd-Jones, 'Interesting Times', in the *International Journal of the Classical Tradition*, vol. 4 no. 4 (spring 1998), 580–613. Lloyd-Jones documents the major studies which have been made of the work and influence of classical scholars such as Wilamowitz, Jaeger, Schadewaldt, Reinhardt, and Fraenkel as well as studies of the relationships between German and American scholarship in the twentieth century. He follows Momigliano in cautioning against over-reliance on the biography of classical scholars as opposed to systematic re-evaluation of their work and its impact (cf. A. Momigliano, 'New Paths of Classicism in the Nineteenth Century', *History and Theory* 21, 1982). Attention both to personal histories and to their relationship with the ideologies of scholarship has emerged in a recent off-shoot of the history of scholarship in which the perspectives of individual scholars are recognized as a shaping force in their work, and by extension in reception studies. A collection of essays on this topic is J.P. Hallet and T. van Nortwick, edd., *Compromising Traditions: the Personal Voice in Classical Scholarship* (London and New York, 1997).

RECEPTIONS OF DRAMA IN LANGUAGES OTHER THAN ENGLISH

Reception of ancient drama is at the centre of international work in both research and practice. In order to identify national and cultural trends and set them in context a good deal of comparative work is necessary. A major study which considers Greek drama from early modern staging of Greek tragedy (*Oedipus the King* in Venice in 1585) until almost the present day is Hellmut

Flashar, *Inszenierung der Antike: das Griechische Drama auf der Bühne der Neuzeit 1585–1990* (München, 1991). Flashar's study contains substantial listings of productions as well as chapters analysing the interaction of Greek drama with German cultural consciousness. Most recently, members of the European Network of Research and Documentation of Greek Drama have produced a number of studies. These range from listings of productions in all languages from 1460 to the present, collected by the Oxford Archive of Performances of Greek and Roman Drama to the data-base of late twentieth-century productions published electronically by the Open University research project on the Reception of the Texts and Images of Ancient Greece in modern drama and poetry (http://www2.open.ac.uk/ClassicalStudies/GreekPlays). A collective publication of the European Network is P. Mavromoustakos, ed., *Productions of Ancient Greek Drama in Europe during Modern Times* (Athens, 1999). This contains articles in Greek, English and French covering research in most European countries. An extensively illustrated work in Greek and English is Spiros Mercouris, ed., *A Stage for Dionysus: Theatrical Space and Ancient Drama* (Athens, 1998). Produced in conjunction with an international exhibition, this covers productions in Greece, Cyprus, Crete, Spain, Italy and Bulgaria. Research in the Czech Republic and Slovakia is documented in English in the special Theatralia edition of *Eirene*, XXXVII, 2001. This important edition of the journal also includes many illustrations. The Centro de Linguas e Culturas at the University of Aveiro in Portugal publishes the proceedings of its research conferences, mainly in French, Portuguese and Spanish, as Agora Supplements (Number 1, 2001, ed. C. Morais, *Máscaras portuguesas de Antigona*; Number 2, 2001, ed. Maria Fernanda Brasete, *Máscaras, vozes e gestos: nos caminhos do teatro classico*). Volumes written in English but which cover an international range of productions include S. Patsalidis and E. Sakellaridou, edd., *(Dis)placing Classical Greek Theatre* (Thessaloniki, 1999) and L. Hardwick *et al.*, *Theatre Ancient and Modern* (Milton Keynes, 2000) (and electronically at http://www.open.ac.uk/Arts/CC99/). Also written in English are studies of reception of drama in the USA, including reference to some international and foreign-language productions, by Karelisa V. Hartigan, *Greek Tragedy on the American Stage: Ancient Drama in the Commercial Theatre, 1882–1994* (Westport CT, 1995) and Amy S. Green, *The Revisionist Stage: American Directors Reinvent the Classics* (Cambridge, 1994).

ABOUT THE AUTHOR

Lorna Hardwick teaches in the Department of Classical Studies at the Open University, where she is Professor of Classical Studies and Director of the Research Project on the Reception of Greek Texts and Images in Modern Drama and Poetry. Her initial academic training was in Ancient History. She also studied European Literature and the History of Ideas and these fields came together to generate her interest in reception studies. She is currently working on the relationships between classical texts and their receptions in post-colonial drama and poetry.